HURT CAPITAL

HURT CAPITAL

ISAAC AMEND

PALMETTO
PUBLISHING
Charleston, SC
www.PalmettoPublishing.com

Paperback ISBN: 979-8-8229-7927-7
eBook ISBN: 979-8-8229-7928-4

For my mother, Alice Wells.

To write is to struggle.

CONTENTS

Chapter 1 1
Chapter 2 4
Chapter 3 8
Chapter 4 17
Chapter 5 31
Chapter 6 35
Chapter 7 42
Chapter 8 48
Chapter 9 54
Chapter 10 62
Chapter 11 68
Chapter 12 74
Chapter 13 83
Chapter 14 89
Chapter 15 93
Chapter 16 104
Chapter 17 112
Chapter 18 117
Chapter 19 123
Chapter 20 131
Chapter 21 133
Chapter 22 135

Chapter 23 144
Chapter 24 150
Chapter 25 155
Chapter 26 160

Acknowledgments 163

1

Dear Mom,

THE PILLS IN my bathroom cabinet are sitting next to each other like fifteen linebackers on a football field. *Bolton. Edmunds. Greenlaw. Wagner. Warner.* The Chiefs are winning, and I haven't even spotted Travis Kelce yet. They're all famous–each single pill bottle–each capsule I need to swallow with orange juice at night. I get the high pulp kind, now, from Trader Joe's, that costs around four bucks. Semi pulp doesn't put the tablets down fast enough. I've got every kind of med imaginable since my first episode ten years ago.

Bipolar has never felt so bad. But it's also never felt so *good.* The mania that lasted for a year last September has crept away, but its high still remains in my head. At least partly. Partially. Essentially. Basically, it was awesome. I celebrated at every turn. Went walking for hours on end, only to feel my breath creeping into my lungs, and out, past midnight, when I dreamt of fairytales and candy cane land and piles of dollars stacked so high in front of Rick Ross. So high that he forgot he sold coke. I forgot he sold coke. I forgot a lot of that year, Mom.

I want to be like Rick Ross one day. I want to star in a song with Drake. Rapping about lemon pepper chicken and taking my celebrity son to French Montessori. I want to be a hustler, a gangster at every turn, a coke warlord just *fiending* for a kingdom. The kingdom I create is in my mind: it's ruled by Dostoevsky and Tolstoy and even Pushkin. I named a cat after Pushkin. Russian writers have never felt so real. I want them to come back from the dead and resurrect themselves–all polished and everything. No wax. I remember visiting Tolstoy's grave with you in Moscow, when henchmen roamed the city at night and CIA officers were prowling the embassy's corridors. I was scared in Moscow. Scared back then. Scared of my female body. But now it's a male one, and I'm a son. I'm your son, Mom. But I'm troubled. Very troubled indeed.

I went to a soccer game again. We are named Footyholics. We played near Logan Circle, in the backyard of a school, and I swear the soccer ball was going to kill me. It hit my head, with a bang–not a whimper–and zoomed past some crust on my earlobes. My black stud almost shook for a bit. I clenched the ring you got me on my index finger. You got it from Delhi, and now I'm remembering things back there as well, when you and I lived in India. But there are many things I still can't remember, Mom. Just trust me on that one. Trust me.

Here's one thing I do remember, though: getting in that car accident with you. In Delhi. You were all up in the front seat, and Helen and I were in the back. And a motorcyclist went clamp on the right window, and his flesh and blood were splayed all near for us to see. He died that day, and I think that's the first time I ever saw you cry. I only saw you cry a second time, when Dad was in Kabul, and you missed him like hell, and Phoebe had a tantrum on the National Gallery steps, and you drove us back home, teary-eyed, and you just sat crying that day, in the DC suburbs. And there was not a damn thing I could do about it.

We lost the soccer game. Footyholics lost. But we grabbed a few beers after, at a place near the traffic circle, where expats and missionaries and bankers were fiending for a beer as well, all alike, just as I was fielding for a kingdom in my head. I swear this city is ruled by sociopaths sometimes. They just crawl around here, like ants around a hill, waiting to wreak havoc.

At the bar we were sitting outside, on a wooden table, and we all ordered some beers and some tacos and stuff. And some burritos with chicken. And I swear I shouldn't drink, but I'm just like your husband–there's nothing that tastes better than alcohol in this world, Mom. But beer is bad for me. It's bad for a guy who thinks a soccer ball is going to kill him. At the restaurant, I spotted a street sweeper brushing away leaves. I suddenly fixated on the sweeper: on his crew cut, his black boots, his leather skin. I thought he was manic for leaves. I also thought the waitress hated Jesus until a cross kissed her neck. I thought many things, Mom, and none of them were true.

2

In Cleveland Park, in the basement of my apartment, I took my medicine again, before bed. Now I switched the names up. I named one after Travis Kelce—how could I not? He was dating Taylor Swift—Queen of the World, Empress of Watch Hill, guardian to the royalties of Anti Hero. I'm the problem, it's me, Mom. I really am the problem.

I took the Lithium and put it in the orange juice and swallowed it whole. Then I named it after another tight end–Mark Andrews. He scored ten touchdowns in 2019. These football players have my *back*. They've got me covered, Mom. You won't have to worry anymore. Worry about my health, the state of my kitchen, dishes piled forever, the state of my laundry room, soiled clothes intact, the state of my bathroom. Kelce and Andrews are protecting me. I'm the football, and they're making me score in the end zone.

At night I think of all the wondrous places you've taken me–or rather–where some of your money has taken me. We went to Italy and to the Duomo, and I've also seen Gucci in Milan. Nothing beats Italian fashion. Some days I dress with a Tiffany's bracelet and corduroys, other days I've salivated onto Hanes shirts because of the Lithium poisoning. Then you know what I do–I call my psychiatrist and ask for a blood test. I'm twenty-nine Mom; I'm not sixty. I'm not doing chemo or radiation or some other godawful treatment. I'm just troubled, that's all. You raised a troubled son.

At night I think of all of the women I want to marry. They have to be beautiful, and smart, and rich–just like you. I swore Freud said that sons marry their mothers. She has to be an ambassador–just like you–or rule the world in some other way. She has to wear a Versace gown at night and read Kant in a diatribe, from the very tippy top of her head to me, at half past noon, when we are feasting on avocado toast and white wine. She has to demand the best out of me–the best grades at Harvard Law, the best income, the best penthouse apartment in Greenwich Village–but she also has to deal with my troubled mind. Who's gonna want to do that, Mom? You're the only one in my life who can put up with me right now. Everyone else shies away, or mutters platitudes and puts their phone up, or walks right on out the door. But not you, Mom. You birthed me, and you love me like none other. So I'm going to find a woman just like you.

She has to have blonde hair, and it has to be straightened, and she has to have graduated from Stanford. And she has to know Russian like the back of her hand. And I'm going to find her–trust me–I'm going to find her before you die. And we're going to have a big, fat wedding (maybe a Jewish affair, with smashed glass, because everyone thinks I'm Jewish anyways), and we're going to honeymoon on St. John's, next to the glimmering green of sea turtles and the tantalizing teal of the Caribbean sea. And all of these alliterations are what make me a literary genius to begin with, and being a literary genius is going to save me from the other perils of the world. At least that's what I think, Mama.

I once fell in love, at first sight, with a woman at a bookstore–I was in my early twenties, just out of college, and she was in her mid-thirties: an older woman to me at the time. We were in

Amsterdam, and she was English–from the UK–and we both accidentally reached for *The Metamorphosis* at the same exact time, because Kafka beckoned to both of us, but then Kafka made our first meeting awkward, because our hands, by the grace of God, touched, and because of that touch, I asked her if it was her first time reading it. She said no, and I said no as well. This woman sported a crop of medium length hair–bordering on blonde, but really brown–and she, it turned out, was a literature professor back on home territory. She asked me why I liked *The Metamorphosis.* I gave a very simple, earnest reply: because Gregor Samsa thought he was a monster but was really not, and because Gregor had a sister whom he loved to death, and that I have a twin who I loved to death as well, and sometimes I felt like a monster in front of Helen, but really wasn't, and that therapists had to tell me this on their couches, next to boxes of toilet paper. I told her that page 35 of *The Metamorphosis* was my favorite page, because there, in that scene, Gregor is staring at a sister from a place of misery and self-hatred, but that he sees his sister as a shining light in the world.

The woman carried all of the typical traits that would attract a man like me: she seemed tough–very tough–despite teaching the liberal arts. In another life, she could have easily commanded a squadron of soldiers in the British army. She was also smart–more gifted than the average Yalie, it so seemed–and this appealed to me, and I could tell right off the bat that she was trying to disguise her intelligence, in the interaction, but that she really knew Kafka better than I did, and I thought that I wouldn't be surprised if she also aced physics in college, and calculus, and all subjects, for that matter.

But her toughness was a green flag, and we chatted for around fifteen minutes, about Kafka, and I brought up Toni Morrison, and then she brought up Shakespeare, and really the conversation was not about literature but about how her mannerisms interacted with mine, and I could tell that she liked me, because she told me that part of me was acting older than my age, and right when she said that–right when she said it–I noticed a gold band on her left forefinger, and she noticed that *I* noticed, and she blushed a bit, and became a bit hesitant in the conversation, and had a blemish on her neck. And she could tell that I liked her, because I started flirting, but she liked me as well, because she subconsciously started to move her wedding band around on her hand, and she didn't want it to be there, and I didn't want it to be there either, and neither of us cared for the ring in that moment. Somewhere back home, she was going to go home to a husband–because she seemed straight–and this husband was going to nurture her, and maybe pay for some of the bills, and maybe pay for the house they lived in, and she would go to bed with him, and not me. But I tried, Mom. I really tried.

In Amsterdam, I finally came to the conclusion that I needed a tough woman who liked literature just as much as I do. I have yet to settle down with this kind of woman.

You raised a literary genius, but you also raised a troubled son. Sometimes the two go together hand in hand–like cotton candy to a fair-goer's body, like cement to the effortless tire of an AMG.

I live in Hurt Capital.

3

THE PILLS IN my bathroom are now named after midfielders. *Beckham. Modric. Gerrard. Iniesta. Lampard. Matthaus.*

Remember how Beckham bends the ball into the net? And remember his first famous kick, against Wimbledon, when he hit it from 57 yards out and past the line? The press couldn't get off of his back after that. Fans were in for a frenzy. The stadium went silent and then erupted into a volcano of applause. Well Beckham's bent kick is going to save my mind from a crash, and his dribbling skills are going to give me some extra dopamine, and his corner kicks are going to get rid of bouts of mania. And when Modric plays, well he's going to play for Croatia, and his goals are going to steer me away from depression. I swear this is going to happen, Mom. I swear it.

Hurt Capital is a curated kind of hell–it's a dungeon in Berlin where hipsters get raped and benzoed to death. Hurt Capital is swords on skin, razor blades to the wrist, blades on the back of a shoulder. I am so comfortable in Hurt Capital that I want to stay here forever, betrothed to this specialized nightmare, as if it cost two dollars more than other chocolate bars at a vending machine. Hurt Capital candy. Hurt Capital for my heart.

Puberty was Hurt Capital. The fat on my legs just didn't cut it. I also had breasts. Not big ones, but not small ones either. In eleventh grade, I felt myself slipping away from my body, drifting away from these legs, arms, torso, and curves. Activities like running and drinking with friends lacked pleasure and felt painful. But no matter how many miles I clocked on the track, I couldn't run away from the dissociation.

I've always wondered what it must feel like to fit in. To be born a girl, and to want to stay a girl, and to do ballet without any effort–seamlessly, long, thin legs reaching for the rooftop. To have a posse of girlfriends, to know that you are straight and only like men, to go to Claire's and enjoy getting your ears pierced, to then wear hoop earrings that you also enjoy, to go shopping at Madewell and try on five jeans that your wealthy parents in DC buy, in Georgetown, to fall in love with a prom date senior year, to have that prom date play lacrosse and then play it in college, to go to college with said prom date, to stay in touch with said girlfriends, and to quit ballet to study history, to intern at museums during the summer, to continue to wear hoop earrings, to join a sorority on campus, to enjoy this sorority, to do sorority squats, to have twenty new friends because of said sorority, to have a boyfriend in a frat, to work at the Smithsonian, to then do a career pivot and work at the MET, in New York, to move to New York and make friends easily in Brooklyn, to get married in the Hamptons to the frat star, after having a bachelorette party at Cape Cod, to have two children with said frat star, to move to Westchester, where he will commute work at a bank and this woman will be a manager at the Museum of Modern Art, to be normal.

Being an identical twin meant that I had a carbon copy next to me at all times. But Helen seemed to be everything I wasn't: she was feminine, she could effortlessly put on mascara without hating it, and she could make other girlfriends at the drop of a pin. Having Helen around meant feeling a constant pressure to conform–and to be a girl. If Helen had to be female, then I had to be female too. So for years, I followed in Helen's footsteps, putting on tank tops, skirts, dresses, blush, and eyeliner. These were the rituals that came naturally to her. And to you, and to Phoebe.

Being a twin was torture, Mom. I felt like I had to replicate everything that Helen did. Everything that Helen said. Everything that Helen wore. I felt like I was etched into some carbon copy of her–a piece of paper that had her imprint on it. I felt like I needed to look like her at every turn.

People would always ask us the same questions as kids. *Do you wear the same dresses? Do you like the same flavor ice cream? Have you kissed the same boy? Is telepathy real?*

The questions felt routine at first, but then annoying. Deeply disturbing. I had nothing in common with Helen, yet others felt we were the exact same. There was no space for me to be trans. No space for me to be a boy. No room for fresh air. No yellow brick road I could walk on my way to manhood.

Helen and Phoebe are grown now, appearing taller and older. People say they look more alike to each other than Helen does to me.

As a result, I grew up in a world that was heavily gendered, perhaps all the more so since I was an identical twin sister. Growing up, outsiders, family, and friends would compare my face to Helen's, our posture, our responses to questions, our clothing, and our sports skills. When Helen and I were young, we pulled a prank on friends, asking them to ask us about our favorite sports team, favorite song, favorite color, and favorite book. Before these games, Helen and I would answer these questions ourselves and recite them identically, in the same way our chromosomes were identical. People were astounded at our matching replies.

We were endlessly compared and slotted together as two in one--a package deal. If you got Helen, you got Isabel. If you befriended Isabel, you likely knew Helen. Helen and Isabel were one in the same--two babies, two toddlers, two girls, two teenagers, and then two young adults heeding the same title: Amend twin.

I always felt like Helen had an easier time being a girl. Boys seemed to like her. Jack Haffner, an American football player at the school in Moscow, dated me, but I only found out that he had a crush on Helen the entire time, after he told her this in the embassy cafeteria.

Helen's hair seemed to flow naturally from her shoulders, and she was slender in a way that I wasn't. Moreover, Helen seemed to actually *enjoy* keeping her hair down, and shaving her calves, and wearing mascara, and painting her nails in pastels. It was second nature for her. And this made me jealous.

Meanwhile, I had a difficult time keeping my hair down, painting my nails, and shaving my calves. I did these things only out of a duty to avoid being bullied in the school cafeteria. If I did become a butch girl, I would not have survived the social scene in Russia. Helen, on the other hand, did seem to survive the social scene, and gracefully so. She was an effortless conversationalist and friend to other girls, and indeed made girlfriends as if it was a hidden talent.

To be a reckless and uninhibited version of normal. To fit in: to fit in smoothly, with elegance, with charm, with not-a-worry-in-the-world, to acquiesce to society's standards, but to do so with grace and enthusiasm, to never rebel against a cause, to never speak up, or talk down, or have to scream at the top of your lungs to get psychiatric care or anything of the like.

You and Dad fit in so well. I don't. Trans people, and trans people who have bipolar, stand out like sore thumbs. I am othered in more ways than one, yet refuse to die by my own hands. Something else will have to kill me: the common cold turned into pneumonia when I am eighty five, or a heart attack at seventy-seven. But not suicide.

Indeed, I won't perish by suicide, and refuse to let any suicidal feelings get the best of me, too. I contemplate, often, whether life is worth living, especially as someone who is a fetish–someone who can never fit into the crowd.

Perhaps normal doesn't really exist–and is just an illusion that we buy into to feel safe. The jury is out.

IN NEW HAVEN ONE summer, during Yale, I worked at a startup to fight ISIS propaganda.

I was unhinged in college, Mom. Totally unhinged. Lunging, arbitrarily, at administrators, fervently writing chaotic rubberish on paper in front of everyone to see, sending non-cogent emails to professors at all hours of the day, going in and out of psychosis from one week to the next, breaking up with friends and then fighting with more people on top of that, and just, generally speaking, not going on that many dates.

I got into any class I wanted, Mom. Many of the professors knew about me because I'm brill–I'm brilliant beyond belief, Mom. I got Charles Hill as my thesis adviser within hours of messaging him.

But I was surrounded by all of these dumb ass students. People who would never get a tattoo in their life. People who were Type A–just straight up dumb asses, if you ask me.

If there's one thing that Yale convinced me of, it's that left-leaning people who worship Hillary Clinton can still be sociopaths. Still be mean girls, mean boys, mean men, mean everything. Bullies at every turn. Sociopaths craving to be the next president of America, the next Fortune 500 CEO, the next

Jamie Dimon of Wall Street, the next Toni Morrison of literature–just–just like me.

Senior society was a bully pit that I should have left right away. My society, Elihu, is meant for left-leaning students who believe in social justice. But left-leaning students in social justice can still treat others horribly, so now I don't trust the political spectrum to be a good determinant of character. I've met right-wing evangelists who treat me like the finest block of gold being traded on the NASDAQ, and communists who slant me at every turn.

One of my closest acquaintances is a Lebanese Christian man who believes in enacting the scripture but who considers me Jesus reincarnate. I don't like political labels anymore. I still think banning abortion is wrong, I think banning gay marriage is heinous, and I think banning sodomy is a symptom of mental illness, but that doesn't stop the fact that some of my closest allies have been conservatives. We find a way to make it work. And I am friends with liberals too–Democrats who want the best for the world.

But some Democrats bite. And choosing your friends based on which party they stand for is borderline foolish. I've been tantalized and teased by enough progressives at Yale to know that one's voting record is no indication of character. In fact, it can be a horrible indication of character. I trust someone's political party to be a good indicator of character as much as I trust Bill Clinton not to ask a woman for a blowjob. And while we're on the matter, Bill Clinton is a horrible Democrat who raped and assaulted women at every turn. JFK was also a sleazy elitist who asked for hundreds of sexual favors in the White House pool. He wasn't the regal prince the press cracked him up to be. Jacquie Onassis was delighted to be out of his grips when she married that shipping tycoon from Greece.

I didn't go to Yale for the social scene, Mom. I didn't go there to schmooze at frats and sororities. I didn't go there for any teatime niceties. I went there to pound out hard literature and meet brilliant professors. And sleep with the occasional man or woman along the way.

Yale was hard, in many ways. I didn't like the people who went there. They seemed too young, too immature, too inexperienced at life. I wasn't myself, at all. I wasn't developed as a person. But I still felt old–too old for any kind of scene. I was past college life. I took the degree and used it for good.

Mom, you raised a soldier. Everything about me is soldier-like: my stare, my gaze, my shoulders, my tone of voice. I take seven pills a day but still find a way to fight, Mama.

As the days went by, and we watched more propaganda, I had day visions of stabbing my breasts with a knife. In these day visions, the flesh of my breasts was parsed apart like it would be in surgery, ripped away, and thrown on the ground. Sometimes, the knives stabbed them so hard that they started to bleed and rot away in the dirt.

Other times, the knives stabbed my breasts lightly, waiting for them to fall. The knives played, in slow circles, with the flesh, until it careened away. The knives were teasing them. In these instances, the flesh came off slowly, in small tranches, in wisps of fat, and the mammary glands fell to the floor, with a faint crash, spilling themselves across linoleum. The knives had done them away and either way, they were gone from my chest for the rest of my days. That's all that mattered.

When I dreamt of them falling into the dirt or onto the linoleum, I became calm again: seduced by the idea of less fat, less curves, and less bras; turned on by a vacancy on my body. It's as if I just climaxed and was soothed by oxytocin. This vacancy was sexy–it's what I ever dreamed of in life–to have less breasts. My heart rate dropped, veins pulsed less heavily, breath intact.

I'm troubled, Mom. I'm trouble, troubled, trouble—troubl—trou–troubled—

Let me tell you about some of my favorite words I use on the shrink couch: *Opulent. Tasteful. Palpable. Tangible. Ostentatious. Euphoric. Smorgasbord.* A smorgasbord of mania and chaotic thinking, doctor.

I also mutter these words to myself, at home, in the bathroom, when I'm standing next to linebackers and tight ends. Travis Kelce is right there on the medicine stand, rooting for me all the way, as if I'm a Kansas City Chief myself. Hell, I could play a whole game if I wanted to, with those guys behind my back. And Taylor Swift would watch on.

Some say to write about being bipolar and trans is to demean yourself. Peg yourself down to a low level in life. One where people will mock you, cajole you, tease you, make fun. Mutter platitudes in your direction, hoping they pierce your heart. But what they don't know is that I will perfect this manuscript so well that its proceeds will pay for a better life–one where I'm not nagging you and Dad for money all the time. Or at least, its impact will put me in a better place in life–a place where I can have a say on literary things on TV, or something of the like.

And then I'll write another book, and another one after that, and I'll win a Pulitzer, and then I might even bag a Nobel. And at that point I can teach a seminar at Harvard and, I don't know, work on some startup out of Boston. I could teach myself how to code, or just use my literary clout to get clout in the entrepreneurial world. And then I'll use my clout to get more things: interviews with Selena Gomez and Mariah Carey, both victims of bipolar themselves. And I might work for a bipolar foundation, or create these Instagram reels that talk about the disease. So Gen Zers can watch. And millenials. And boomers.

I'll become so famous that I'll have a house on the Hills, in LA, next to Drake and the Kardashians. If I'm lucky, Kanye will show up, unannounced at my door, with a big, four cheese pizza in hand. He'll be manic off of an episode and will beg me to give him twelve dollars for the pizza in exchange for him singing "Real Friends" and handing me those damn slices of bread. Then Kanye and I will both do a little dance in LA–in the Hills–and we're going to sing from the top of our lungs about what it's like having bipolar. Kanye will make the beat, and he'll produce the song, and hell, I'll write the lyrics–but Kanye can write them too, because *My Beautiful Dark Twisted Fantasy* was one of the best albums of all time. Actually, it was the best album of all time. Better than *Take Care* and *Astroworld.*

Does anyone have real friends in this world? I'm not yet convinced they exist. Helen, your daughter and my twin, is the closest friend I have. She heard my breath in the womb, and was there right before they took me to NICU with Dad. Helen knows every beating pulse underneath my skin, and can tell that I'm unwell from two oceans away. At night I quietly wonder what life would be like if she's gone. *Sullen. Morose. Depressing.* Utterly catastrophic.

Cis people don't understand the privilege they're born with. Most women I know don't have to worry about going into public bathrooms. They don't have to worry about stalkers and creepers at every turn. They don't understand what it feels like to walk into a men's room and calculate every move so that no man around you catches you being trans and can stab you or kill you at worse.

What is life without another half? Without her other half, would there even be life to begin with? Probably not.

4

THE PILLS IN my toiletry bag are now swimmers. *Phelps. Ledecky. Spitz. Lochte.* There is nothing like the curvature of Michael's arms to remind me that I am safe. His shoulders and biceps and triceps and elbows will save me from mania. His thumbs are hugging me tight, wishing for better days. Katie Ledecky, who hails from just around the corner in DC, is screaming my name. She's chanting *Isaac!* at a national meet. There are eight competitors lined up in the water, and they're all going to do the butterfly. The hardest stroke. Their torsos will oscillate as if carrying golden wings and their legs will kick like dolphins. They'll be thinking of me all race long: they'll be thinking of my health, my spirit, my *joie de vivre*, my happiness. Their hard work will steer my mind clear of sadness. I won't be morose anymore. I'll be content, joyous, pleased. I'll be myself again. They've got my back like none other, Mom–just trust me on that. Just like *you* have my back.

THIS IS WHAT MANIA feels like: imagine a generator–a massive generator–one that can power an entire hospital if there's a power outage. Now imagine that generator emitting energy at the speed of light, and having that energy flow through your body like none other. There are inevitable symptoms of having this much energy in your body. The first is that you can't control your body sometimes, because there is such a surplus of energy, that you feel the need to walk all the time, do jumping jacks at random hours of the day, lift weights for hours on end, and vacuum at midnight, nonstop–just vacuuming to and fro, like it's no one's business. There is so much energy in the body that you might slap a weight on top of another weight, then feel like lifting the treadmill at breakneck speed.

Another symptom is constant night sweats. When mania is truly present in the body–and I mean truly present for days and weeks on end, without stopping–you will sweat profusely at night, so much so that your spouse becomes bothered with the salty sheets, and feels the need to wash them every other day. There is so much sweat, in fact, that many change of shirts and pants are necessary, so I keep around two dry shirts on the bedside table, and one replacement set of pants. At two a.m., or even three a.m., or four, when I wake up to soaked clothes, I will take the drenched shirt and wring it out in the bathroom sink, so much so that sweat comes out in slight troves, like a small fountain at any nearby plaza in Florence or Rome. It's laughable, almost, how much sweat appears, as if it were a running trough of water.

The third symptom is racing thoughts–during the beginning phase of mania, the thoughts only race a bit, but then they quicken up as the months pass by. And this is one of the scariest of symptoms, because if thoughts race too much, then basic chores, like doing the dishes or laundry, become unachievable, because one is sequestered to their bed, waiting for the thoughts to get slower. This is the beginning of madness, and I tinker on madness all the damn time. At the tail end of mania, the thoughts are too quick to handle–so a medical intervention becomes necessary, and one is required to go to the hospital, or to a clinic, or to rehab, as I fondly did.

The fourth symptom of mania is grandiosity–and I mean grandiosity with everything you do. Vacuuming the clean floor at midnight? I'm the best vacuum artist in the world, and deserve to enter a competition for vacuuming, and I'm going to win first place. Learning how to code Python? I'm the best coder in the world, and will code next to the ranks of Bezos and Musk someday.

Because of all of this excess energy, one is tempted to do many things. I happened to write two poetry books. So naturally, I thought these books were going to win Pulitzers. And surprise surprise–they didn't.

I WAS MANIC FOR a year straight. Twelve months. Those months were the best of my life. I was twenty seven, and the world was a big Chilean oyster cracked in half to offer me riches. The mania crept in slowly at first. It started with a dream: another girl I loved (an heiress) was kissing me. Profusely. In Central Park. I woke up on a high, and went walking for three hours straight, daydreaming of ways to seduce her. *Creative genius.* That night, I sweated profusely in my sleep. I had to replace the first shirt with a second, and the second shirt with a third. I wrung out the third one in the bathroom sink, and splashes of salty water came barreling down. It was a nightmare and a fancy vision all at once: too much sweat but a crescendo of a high.

Confidence spilled through the gates of my heaven. A confidence I had never felt before: a euphoria beholden to the recesses of my mind. Suddenly, the urge to write was born. I started crafting new sentences.

her voice broke at midnight like a cracked auger on the beach
it was a cry wrapped in newsprint, asking the remains of the day
to forgive her tongue

let me whisper in the murk of the juniper; at Mount Heron there
are only three skipper
butterflies who will make me weep.

I took a vacuum, and started sweeping the floors with it. It wouldn't go fast enough, so I sped it across the wood, hoping that dust would not prevail. It took in dirt slowly, then quickly at first. The sound came roaring into the background like a Boeing jet on departure. It wouldn't get out of my ears. I turned it off.

Then I took my nailbeds, and scratched them vociferously. *Vociferously*. Another word from the hidden dictionary. They started to cripple, then bleed, then the blood turned into crimson scabs. Then I scratched the scabs away, until those bled some more, and turned into a second scab.

I proceeded to go on *another* walk through the Virginian woods where I dreamt of scenarios in which I could woo the heiress to my dinner table. One involved singing *Lean Back* with Fat Joe and Remy Mafia at a club in downtown DC. Another involved saying the f-word thirty-nine times on the Joe Rogan podcast. And yet *another* scenario involved me leading an orchestra at the Kennedy Center to the tunes of the Harry Potter soundtrack, waving a wand as my baton. *Diagon Alley* and the *Gringott's Vault* had never felt too real.

All of these visions–these fantasies–are just grandiose thoughts. They're what the psychiatrist warned against. But the fact that I'm having these visions makes me somewhat of a creativ–a creative genius. Every thought I think comes with a motion picture. My close friend just slept with my ex-wife? Bam. Zoom in to a shot of him seducing her in his condo. They're drinking tea–because they're too wholesome for their own good–and talking about the weather at Reagan airport. She has to pick up an aunt from a flight soon, but wants to lay in bed with him first.

The thought paralyzes me, then freezes me some more, then makes me somewhat enraged. The world is run on adrenaline and pheromones. There's no turning back. No thinking twice. People suck. Friends are disloyal. Earth is a dystopia. Forget about the friend. And forget about the ex-wife. This is what you would want me to do, yet I'm too scared to voice these fears to you. You'll think I'm juvenile, an adolescent, a teenager at heart. A boy who can't stomach bad news. You want me strong for even worse news–news about sickness in our family, or death, or the loss of an inheritance. This is the stuff that *really* matters, Mom. Not romantic dalliances on the side.

Because of the mania, in my head, I picture each one of my friends rolling around in a wheel. It's like a hamster wheel, except they're the hamster, and they're human, and they're full of chaos, just like me. And they might be screaming, or mouthing nonsense into the air, and they're anxious, but excited. Then I picture people in my life with their arms folding into two, crashing to the ground. I picture their legs bending into weird contort—contor—contortions—another word from the hidden dictionary. I hope that these strange pictures in my mind won't materialize into any kind of hallucination, but that's only happened twice to me before, and I know I'm not thinking logically.

At the height of my mania, I also pictured two scary people in my head. The first was a woman saying "sixth sense" over and over again inside my mind—but not any kind of tangible voice though that I'm wrongly hearing. Just an image of her. The second is a skinny man in sunglasses saying "stranger things". Again, not an actual voice, because I can't hear anything—just a film in my mind. These characters that my brain has made up are not any form of hallucination but rather people that my brain has fictionalized and because I daydream all day long I daydream of them. I'm convinced that all of these obscure visualizations the mania has summoned make me, to some extent, deranged. But I learn to live with the derangement and as the mania is broken by the lithium, and as my mind recovers more and more by the day, the visualizations start to leave my mind entirely. When they do, I become convinced that I'm getting better.

I still question the visualizations, though. I wonder if they are the beginning of a potential hallucination—that, if I was extremely unwell, would somehow show up in hallucination form. If, someday, I would somehow see these people as real things, when they weren't. That thought scares me, so I put it aside for the time being and don't tell my psychiatrist about it.

In February of 2023, I went to a rehab facility in New York City to break my mania. While rehabs are technically meant for drug addicts, I still had a big enough addiction to alcohol—and a reliance on Xanax as a sleep med—to warrant a rehab stay. I also chose rehab because I was avoiding the psych ward, as psych wards can be notoriously unpleasant and hard to deal with. They can lock you in there, and the general setting of most psych wards is less comfortable than the upscale rehab center covered by insurance.

When I checked into rehab, I told the staff that I was drinking either a bottle of wine or a six pack of beer each night, sometimes coupled with one or two glasses of scotch, and then taking all of my bipolar meds, in addition to Xanax and a drug called Quetiapine, to sleep. I told the staff that during this period of heavy drug use, I would also occasionally wake up to find myself having a hard time breathing, and that breathing when I took all of these meds together was a big concern of mine. I also told them that

I had been manic for one year straight, and demanded a lithium intervention as soon as possible—immediately, urgently, right away. From what I had read, I knew that lithium would most likely zap my mania away, but I had to wait several days before starting the drug, due to blood tests and logistical mistakes.

After about 10 days, the rehab staff was finally able to administer me lithium. Both the biological and behavioral differences that happened three days after taking lithium are almost too profound to mouth. After about two days, I was finally able to sleep for 9 hours straight, without any medication needed. Finally—finally—I stopped sweating at night too. Gone were the days when I had to take two shirts to put on my bedside table, and gone were the days where I'd wring out the sweat from these shirts. I was also able to nap, on my own accord, about once each day, which was also unheard of.

My speech also slowed. Instead of talking quickly in abrupt, crazed sentences, and instead of manically drawing thunderstorms on A4 paper with pink and purple crayons, I was able to sit in one chair for thirty minutes straight and read a book, without twitching—without fidgeting, without moving chaotically, without yelling at someone. Helen noticed a difference in my voice on the phone with her. She said I was speaking more steadily, and that I sounded way more calm than before. She said I seemed more well, just by the conversations I was able to lead. The rehab staff also noticed a marked difference in my behavior: they said I was more centered, more grounded, and just less quick to do things and say things in general. They said I was now living with a normal amount of energy, and that the lithium had, indeed, worked.

In addition to these changes, the lithium also gave me one symptom that I did not foresee happening at all: it made me more socially inhibited. This was a good thing, because prior to its use, I was not socially inhibited at all. For several years—or, in fact,—ever since the bipolar came knocking through the door of my body—I was quick to say things that were gauche, bold, and just generally inappropriate. The lithium took all of that away. I suddenly found myself more polite in conversations, slightly more reserved—but in a good way—and more aware of social conventions when talking to others. How one drug can magically make me better at teatime conversations with Indian aunties beats the living hell out of me—and I will never fully understand modern pharmacology. But it works, and medicine is a good thing, and—contrary to what many other bipolar patients do—I have never gone off my meds, nor do ever plan on doing so. Despite missing the high of a year full of mania, I take lithium, and other pills, religiously, as if they are my second church, standing next to the first one, which is alcohol. The only sin I commit in my church of bipolar is, indeed, belonging to the other church of alcohol. Besides drinking, I am a successful bipolar patient: I attend therapy regularly, take my pills, get enough sleep, and exercise each day. I also am vocal about the disease to friends and loved ones, so much so that they can counsel me through depressive ruts and other hard times. Most people I confide in generally treat me well, and don't run away from the disease. In writing this book, Mom, I'm not running away from it either.

Because I was manic for a year, there were different stages to the development of my mania. The positive effect of the mania can be mapped on a graph as a line that has a consistent negative slope alongside the positive-positive x-y axes. Here is a graph: Let's just make the equation to the line $y = -0.5x$. As an absolute value, I like 0.5 as a slope, because it suggests a slow, steady decline—not a rapid or catastrophic fall in the state of things.

Towards the end of my mania, in the last third of it, I experienced racing thoughts. The racing thoughts crept in slowly at first, but then made their presence known like a tiger that just barraged through the inner sanctums of my mind. And barr—barra—-barrage is another word from the hidden dictionary. Webster says it means to bombard someone with something. I guess I was right. Out of all of the symptoms of mania, racing thoughts—and disorganized thoughts—was probably the scariest of them all. I'm trying to find a good metaphor to explain racing thoughts. I think I can make one using guns. Picture yourself standing at a shooting range, and being given a shotgun by an instructor to shoot at a target. The target is a blue cut out body, and you have to shoot around twenty times to make your mark. The shotgun isn't double barreled, so you have to reload it every time you want to shoot again. Over the course of thirty minutes, you methodically shoot, load, and then reload the shotgun so your twenty shots are done properly. Picture each shot as a thought that goes through your mind. With a shotgun, the thoughts are going slowly—methodically—and on time.

Another scary symptom of the bipolar is pressured speech. Pressured speech is a phenomenon in which one talks faster than usual, and might jump around topics, with little awareness of their verbal chaos. At its worst, pressured speech can involve a stutter, or even confusion among words—so instead of saying a feeling I had was "positive", I might say the word "position" instead, which makes no sense. In my experience, pressured speech happens a lot towards the end of mania, after many months of battling it. At the very beginning, it is present less. Towards the end of a months-long manic episode, pressured speech is basically a threat in every conversation I hold with people and even after the mania is over, pressured speech is hard to get rid of. It lingers even after the lithium intervention, and can linger for months more to come. Certain things that help reduce pressured speech is getting enough sleep—and in fact just a tad bit more sleep than usual. If I'm usually getting 7 hours, I might aim for

8.5 or 9, making sure that my REM cycle is activated properly so the sleep I'm receiving is deep, and not light. Another thing that drastically reduces pressured speech is not consuming any drugs—not drinking, not smoking weed, not doing any white lines. But again, Mom, the first church I belong to is That of Alcohol. It is my only health flaw.

In conversations with friends, I would find myself stuttering to a pretty big extent. At a brewery, when talking about a soccer game, I said it was "s—s—sp—spectacular". The s just couldn't come out. I thought the corner kick was "a—a—ama—amazing". The a had a hard time making an appearance. Friends would also point out that my speech was slurred. *Different. Undecipherable.* One day, my landlord asked me to repeat an entire sentence. She couldn't understand a word I was saying.

At one point, when I was very unwell, I heard my twin sister's voice in my head—not outside of it. She was saying, over and over again, that I was, indeed, unwell. "Isaac you're not well, Isaac you're not well, Isaac you're not well..." Her voice started playing so loudly in my head that I had to take sleep meds to sleep it off. This is a cognitive symptom called looping that I never wanted to experience again, but did in rehab. In the moment, I thought I was going crazy—and it certainly felt like it. But trauma, when not addressed properly, can cause these very atypical symptoms to happen–as in, it can cause looping voices in your head to happen.

In rehab, I experienced looping again. Another patient in the facility—who just happened to be my roommate—composed an acoustic song commemorating the rehab center. It was funny, and offered the patients—and the staff—some comedic relief. We sang about having to take Seroquel to go to sleep, and about taking muscle relaxers to fall asleep again when we woke up at 3am from our roommate's snoring. The roommate who made the song was a bright, energetic queer man who uplifted all of the patients in the facility. Right before he left, we gathered on the top floor of the facility to have a communal singalong session with staff and patients alike. Just a few days later, the song got stuck in my head in a very strange way in the bathtub, before bed. It started looping over and over in my brain, until I just couldn't get it out of there. It became loud—louder than usual—and something that was not only annoying, but disturbing. That night, I took sleep meds to get rid of the looping, and had my biggest trauma dream yet, in which I woke up at 2am screaming at the top of my lungs. My heart was pounding in my chest, and this night—but only this night—I was sweating profusely once more.

Allow me, upon second revision of this manuscript, to detail one more symptom of my bipolar. Now this is perhaps the scariest one of them all–scarier than my occasional twin's voice running through my head, scarier than seemingly unending mania, and scarier than racing thoughts. I call them "psychotic one offs". Let me paint a picture for your: I'm at a gas station somewhere near the Outer Banks, several months after my mania has subsided. I take my Ford Fusion to a gas canister and start filing it up with liquid. I lock the car and take my wallet to the convenience store where I buy a pack of peanuts and Coca Cola - I don't drink the diet this kind. But all of a sudden, when I'm talking to the cashier behind the counter, she's mouthing these abnormal thoughts to me through her voice. She (a cisgender woman) is telling me that she was an alcoholic in Russia, and that she's secretly a trans man - that she's not a woman but a man. Surely what she's saying isn't true, and is a concoction being spun up in my own head. When she's mouthing these nonsensical things to me that surely aren't based in reality–and in any semblance of what she's actually saying–I become stressed beyond relief. I go back to my Ford sedan and forget to unpeg the gas tube from the car, so that when I drive off the gas tube hits the car of a military veteran.

Still stressed, the veteran can tell my heightened state, and we plea to settle the minor car brush out of pocket. Ultimately, I pay him a few hundred dollars out of pocket to settle his debt, and he willfully agrees, trusting what I have to say. But the stress of the situation lingers on for weeks and potentially months to come. How can my brain be so feeble as to not decipher the reality in front of me? As to warp, as if I'm in some kind of hallucinatory phase, the words and actions and gestures coming out of another person in front of me? This, in many ways, is the worst end of the bipolar. It makes me question my sanity, hours later, on a beach in the Outer Banks, as the waves roll to and fro across my ankles, dotting them in pebbles and random tidbits of sand that cling to my wet bones. My mind looks across the Atlantic and thanks God for the well built house that my parents afforded for my sisters and I to stay in, but I also question God's spinning of my mind. Did he take my mind into one of an alternate universe? One where reality doesn't come knocking at my doorstep; one where I can't, after all of this time and effort, decipher reality for the life of me. And that indeciphering of reality - of experiencing out of body experiences and quasi hallucinations - is what really puts me in overdrive, devising a twelve step plan to get better right away - to not be stuck in this nightmares where I'm seeing things and hearing things that aren't real. Moreover, the "psychotic one off", as my doctors call it, could be emblematic of previous psychotic one offs that I have experienced in the past. For instance, in Iowa, in a small university town, I experienced a cashier at a hotel saying she was doing meth. But she said she was doing meth in this robotic tone–the same tone that the gas station cashier declared that she was a transman and alcoholic from Russia. These realities become thwarted. Thwarted beyond belief. And that's what scares me–that at the relatively tender age of 30, I could be losing my mind. Maybe not losing my mind permanently, but in small bouts and doses–ones I am able to recover from with strengthening antipsychotic drugs like Risperdal and countless psychotherapy and therapy sessions.

I don't want to experience a psychotic one off again. They peg me as a mad man - a lunatic - a patient embroiled with flirtations with reality and not-reality. I would rather be manic for six months straight than have a psychotic one off. But the psychotic one offs are treatable, indeed, with therapy sessions that remind me they are just a symptom of the disease festering inside of my brain, and it will always fester, but I can control its chaos with less alcohol consumption, less drugs, more exercise, more doctors sessions, and better friends.

THE AMNESIA IS KILLING me. I have no way of knowing what happened during my first psychotic episode. I don't know if it lasted for days, weeks, or months. I plan on finally asking you tomorrow, or sometime next week.

When amnesia hits, the body and mind can suffer in unforeseen ways in the present moment. A lack of remembrance of several weeks of your life, especially when so young, can induce a bizarre psychological state. I can't properly describe this phenomenon–it's hard to put into words.

My brain sometimes feels fuzzy–like I can't identify certain emotions and thoughts. Other times, I feel super charged–like these previously unidentifiable emotions are on high alert, exercising recklessly on row machines and treadmills and the hamster wheels inside the head.

I'm worried that if I open up to anyone about my amnesia they won't understand it, or run away, or both. The amnesia can affect how you speak. How you think. How you feel. And the scariest part is–you have no way of knowing how it's controlling the present moment.

All of this is uncontrollable–the bipolar is uncontrollable. It swims through the body and does freestyle strokes next to neural synapses. It plunges underwater–into the organs–and makes them crippled. It grinds the teeth at night.

5

THE PILLS IN the bathroom are NBA players. I'm sick of the crust the pills leave in my mouth, I'm sick of their acidic taste, and I'm sick of their bulky feel. I'm sick of buying high pulp orange juice just to get them down. I want to drink normal orange juice for a change. So just let me make them NBA players, for once. Let me get my wish. Let them dissipate into thin air and turn into monsters dunking a ball. Let me make them shooting stars with a meteoric rise–celebrity athletes that push me all the way to a better world. I'm going to name them after the Lakers, because I've always dreamt of sitting next to Adele and Justin Bieber in the stands in LA. Next to other celebs.

Here is my pill roster: *Lebron. Davis. Russell. Kuzma. Schroder.* First things first, Russell is going to pass the ball to Kuzma. Then Kuzma is going to fake a Toronto Raptor and pass to James. Then James is going to take the ball out to the three point line, and dunk from just a few feet inside of that. And in the meantime, Drake is going to be in the stands as well, because he's a sponsor of Toronto, but he's going to clap in favor of James, because he's so in awe with his willpower. Just let me have Drake clap for James, please. And that's going to be the play for the night, and as the dunk is made, *Hold On I'm Going Home* is going to play in the stadium. And women are going to swoon and kiss their lips at the front row. And because that's going to happen, my bipolar will suddenly be cured, and I won't worry about having to take these goddamn pills for the rest of my life. I won't have to worry about lithium tests, and going to any hospital, and the risk of dialysis. I won't have to worry about mania, and I won't have to worry about a sinking depression, and I won't have to worry about the fear of seeing or hearing things. Just make me not worry–Lakers–make me not–make me not worry for a bit.

You conceived us in Tajikistan, just as a Civil War had largely come to rest. You found out you had twins six months into the pregnancy, when an ultrasound at the Japanese Embassy told you so. So you flew back to DC with Dad, and a bag of Tajik bread–riddled with small pebbles inside the dough. Not the kind of pebbles Kanye would sell in Hidden Hills. In a pizza standing sonically next to *The Life of Pablo.*

Perhaps Tajikistan did a number on you. Maybe the stress during your pregnancy is what made me somewhat crippled. I'm not sure. I don't think any country really ruined you–not Russia, not Saudi Arabia. You are an ocean that puts up with the worst surfer waves. I don't think you could be ruined, ever. I think moving to all of these countries every two or three years made me less social, because I kept losing friends. They just disappeared into the fray–into the horizon–like linebackers gone astray from a football field. I lost Emily, Sasha, Kristina, Ellen.

My worldview is built on cynicism, starting from the day I was 12, and landed in Russia (FSB spies, surveillance, etc. etc. the world around us was cold in Russia–both in the physical and metaphorical sense).

In Russia, there was something nice about having girls as friends. Being a bro is overrated–just me on that one. Remember when Helen and I joined the Moscow soccer team? Tournaments were in Budapest and Bucharest and Warsaw. On trips we shoveled ice cream in student teacher lounges and prowled shopping malls in Bucharest, scrutinizing dresses at H&M and Zara. In the city, Russian women were "fitful," people would say. High, black leather boots and white tunics during the summer, mink fur in January and loud red lipstick all the time. Vodka in precious shot glasses and black caviar on blinis.

The Novy Arbat was packed with nightclubs–drunkards would come out at 8 a.m. on weekdays, some with bottles of Stolichnaya. Helen and I, then 13, raced to a kiosk against your will in one of the six-lane avenue's underpasses, buying Redd's beer. We were not of age for alcohol, but that didn't matter–only that we were tall enough to reach the counter.

I'm going to call booze the B-word here–because that's just what it is, the b-word, upper or lower case. It's not worth saying out loud because it could trigger me to pound a whole bottle of vodka in one night. Mom, I believe I started my addiction to B–let me just call it B–in Russia. The first taste of alcohol I ever had (besides church wine) was when I was 12 and in Rosinka. Remember Rosinka? The suburb on the outskirts of Moscow where all of the oil kids lived. Kids with *parents* who worked for big oil, to be precise. So I had this sip of vodka–it could have been Stolichnaya–and the way it burned on my tongue and in my liver was too much of a high to even describe.

And I never told you this, but I started sneaking a bottle of your red wine into my room some nights, and I drank about half of it on my own, just staring at the Russian parliament outside my window. And then I would buy some cigarettes–from that same underpass–usually Camels, or Marlboros, and I'd smoke one–just one–each night, because I hated my body, and I hated what it was doing to my mind. I knew that my messed up body would twist my mind into one contorted heap of a mental mess when I got back to the states to finish high school. I didn't want to go back to the states. I wanted to live in Russia-land forever, home to soccer and shopping and black limos and walks on the Arbat. Suburban Virginia was full of too many *soccer moms* and *minivans*–relics of moderate prosperity near DC boulevards.

I'm not sure if Dad liked Moscow. One winter, he bought a lamp that would illuminate our skin and faces to save us from seasonal depression. Dad seemed somber in Moscow. *Downcast. Despondent. Full of sorrow.* Sometimes he seemed grim, matching the sweeping cold winters that would freeze our eyelids shut if we forgot to dry ourselves fully from a shower. These winters were barren and cruel–us schoolkids barely saw thirty minutes of sunshine each day, and would clamor outside during recess just to catch a ray. It was worth the hustle.

We both know I'm not meant to be Dad's son, Mom. He's Type A. I'm chaotic. He sold missiles in corporate offices. I lose money by self publishing poetry books. He counts his ties and jackets. Organizes the papers in his office in geometric fashion, with nothing but 90 degrees angles allowed on the desk. He wakes up at 4:30. I wake up at 4pm when I'm unemployed. He runs. I vape and drink B to my heart's content. He owns a farm. I don't know the difference between John Deere and an oak tree. Dad's functional. I'm *dys*functional, Mom.

My hands are bloodied. Things from the past are coming back to haunt me, but there's no turning back–there's no running away any more.

6

KEYA AND I end up living together in Fairfax, Virginia. Her mom, Rashmi, is sick with pancreatic cancer. It is terminal. From 9am to 9pm, Keya cooks for her parents and takes care of her mother at their family house. From 9pm to 9am, we spend the night with each other, sloshing IPAs and raspberry cocktails, watching Omar, a gay robber, kiss a man and thieve crack dens on *The Wire,* or Millenials dancing around on *Too Hot to Handle,* these six-foot-three models and Brits guiding our evening. Our nights together become an exercise in touching base again--after hours and hours spent caring for hospital trips, chemotherapy injections, and pain medications.

The world becomes a bit darker from her mom's sickness. Keya often cries herself to sleep in bed, and reaches over for an arm and shoulder to hold. But the darkness has a strange way of illuminating the brighter things in our routines, as if we are clinging to positive memories a bit more desperately, and cherishing them altogether. We start growing basil plants in our patio, and briefly foster two dogs from the local Fairfax shelter.

Carla is a four-month-old puppy who races from corner to corner when we zig zag across the floor. Her head is the size of our hand, and when she nestles in bed she takes on the shape of a French croissant. The other dog, Caitlyn, is catatonic and traumatized for one week, scared of human interaction. She doesn't venture outside, and sits behind recycling bags or sofas. After a week of care, she ventures out and licks my arm, then spends all hours of the day cuddled in my lap, seeking affection.

In addition to *The Wire* and *Too Hot to Handle*, we watch *Bridesmaids* and *Mamma Mia*, and I occasionally indulge Keya in the action movies that have defined my adolescence and young adulthood: the Jason Bourne series, *Syriana, Zero Dark Thirty, American Sniper, The Hurt Locker, Blood Diamond, Munich,* and *Body of Lies.* I don't get her to watch all of these things, but she makes fun of Jason Bourne and *Homeland,* where Carrie Matheson grips on to Russian handlers and Brody, a marine turned congressman who spies for the other side.

Jessica Chastain finds a bin Laden courier named Abu Ahmad. Bradley Cooper wards off the enemy with single bullets as a SEAL. Jason Bourne tries to find out who he is. In the 1970's, Eric Bana avenges the Palestinians who murdered eleven Isrealis at the Munich Olympics.

I try to indulge Keya in the action movies that made up my childhood: *Jason Bourne*, *Syriana*, *Zero Dark Thirty, American Sniper, The Hurt Locker, Blood Diamond, Munich, Body of Lies,* and *Homeland.* In these shows and movies, CIA agents are sent to Pakistan, spooks are shooting AK's at enemies in Kabul, and smugglers like Leonardo DiCaprio are hiding diamonds in the mouths of goats as he crosses the Congo's border (fact check this). Villages and women are pillaged and terrorists are sent running; Carrie Matthison spots a traitor in Congress and watches as he's hung from a crane in Tehran. DiCaprio makes another appearance in Jordan--a place we know well--and becomes great friends with the leader of the *mukhabarat*, who tortures foes in dungeons.

Keya doesn't seem interested in this world--or, at the very least, makes fun of it. She thinks Carrie Matthison is a bit maniacal--too self-centered, too wrapped up in her own CIA drama. Too narcissistic. Maybe too bipolar.

We watched Jason Bourne last night, and there is something so illuminating about his struggle. Somewhere, deep down, I feel it too–I feel Bourne's struggle. There are memories that have only caught up with me recently–memories of traumatic events far, far away in the past. And they appear in my dreams, and then I go to certain spots in far away cities to relive those dreams, as if standing near a college dorm room or walking the streets of New Haven will somehow rekindle even more repressed memories, but then this becomes a hare-brained scheme–something that a fool would seem to do, or a mad man, but I pro–I promise, there are more memories to uncover. Some of them show up, occasionally, in fretted nightmares, and then disappear again, and slowly I'm starting to put together the fragments of what once was. But slowly, Mom. Not with speed. Very slowly.

Keya thinks Jason Bourne is a privileged white guy who has nothing better to do than complain about his memory and the massive wads of cash he's given in a Swiss vault. I don't show Keya *Blood Diamond* for a second time because it would scare her off--the amputation of child arms and blood diamonds from Sierra Leone--Zambians filled with rage and furor; smugglers getting shot and journalists all the while falling in love with them, these characters of murky morals who report to arms dealers in vineyards outside of Cape Town. The dealers--often white South Africans and colonels and generals--control the flow of arms in Africa, and reap millions of dollars along the way.

The hero of *Syriana*, a man called Bob Baer who is played by George Clooney, was rumored to work with Mom and Dad in Tajikistan, back in the day. George Clooney had to gain weight for the role, and Bob is known as a crazy man within the agency, railing against the CIA's bureaucracy. The CIA accused Bob of trying to assassinate Saddam Hussein without telling them. True or not, Bob denies this.

Indeed, Saddam's daughter lives in a stucco-walled house near the Amman embassy compound in the neighborhood of Abdoun. Jordanians secretly, or not so secretly, actually love Saddam Hussein. Saddam, despite being a dictator, brought stability to the region. He warded off enemies near and far. Saddam was a killer, but at the same time brought many people peace.

Keya does not seem privy to this world--nor does she really want to be. Instead, we spend our time dreaming of going to the beach in Goa, of visiting her grandmother--her *Ammah*--in Hyderabad, or of crossing sand deserts in Rajasthan, where Helen and Phoebe and I used to play among fortress walls. Keya and I speak of fall in Montreal and spring in the US Virgin Islands, where rum flows freely from coconut coffers at tiki bars in Trunk Bay. When we visit Trunk Bay, we think that dolphins may leap in the distance, and that sting rays may be circling nearby. There is an underwater museum that Keya snorkels over--remnants of fish and other amphibians living in the water. The arrows guide her around the rocks, and she could care less about Jason Bourne or Abu Ahmad.

In Fairfax, at night, when the lights have gone from dim to dark, and when our foster animals were put to sleep after a few whimpers, Keya seems to tuck herself away in a world uninhabited by me. There are things she doesn't tell me--thoughts she doesn't articulate, feelings she doesn't emote, or memories she chooses not to share. Her body is slumped and curved, forming half of an oval shape on the bed sheets. She dreams in one world and lives in the next, hiding things for fear of getting hurt or stabbed by heartbreak.

Tucked away somewhere in Keya's mind is a whole array of pictures, flashing images, dialogue with friends, and past doings that she keeps under wraps. This repertoire of untold feelings keeps her silently happy. If we were to break up, she would open up this world she has kept away from me, and it would eventually outshine the depression and grief she would feel from leaving our relationship.

I don't blame her for not telling me things. She has to keep these treasures close to her heart—memories and prior experiences that light up her world--memories and experiences that she does not tell me about.

In her dreams, I wonder if she thinks about her mom's sickness, or the pangs of violent memories during childhood, or the streets of Hyderabad or Mumbai where her first cousins and aunties live with packs of street dogs, the majesty of the Taj Mahal, delicious street food only costing a couple bucks, dialects such as Tamil, tech universities that spoon out the best and brightest software engineers, *mehndi,* and a BJP government that borders on fascist. Modi, India's president, is, indeed, like a Trump 2.0. Albeit smarter, more modest, and more reserved.

Keya might not think of any of these things, instead relegating herself to our current world in northern Virginia--IPA's at Devil's Backbone Brewery, pints at Auld Shebeen, novels taken out from the Fairfax library, walks alongside the Lincoln Memorial, boat tours on the Potomac, where the waters are mostly filled with dirt and slime, but waters that nonetheless reflect the Jefferson Memorial and Washington Monument.

Perhaps these things remind her of her mother--and so by dreaming of them, she is also dreaming of Rashmi, of the perennial light she cast over the family, her care, through ginger tea and hot water pockets, and the close attention she paid towards her daughter's fate.

Mothers are irreplaceable. We all know this. Very few things can break the love a mother has for their child, and very few people can replace that bond. Keya is afraid that she will not find this repository of care in anyone else, for the rest of her life. She tells me, at night, that she is worried that her mother was one of two people who only really knew her, for her life's entirety, from Seattle to DC.

But perhaps over time, Keya will learn to see her mother in the people inhaling and exhaling around her--the friends she meets for coffee, the relatives that flock in and out in small troves in the Fairfax house, the gift packages from aunties and well wishes from distant uncles.

Maybe Rashmi will live on in all of us, I like to think.

KEYA AND I STILL spend time together, at her house, and her voice is as sing-song as ever–just like Rashmi's–Rashmi who died. There is something twistedly precious about the first time a loved one passes away. Rashmi was the first person I've seen die firsthand–I saw her before the diagnosis, for years, happy, among the sands on Chincoteague beach, and then I saw her right after the diagnosis, and then I saw her battle the cancer during chemo, and then we all saw the clinical trial, and how her hair grew back in curls–black curls–and not white–and then we saw her barely able to breathe, and then we saw her pass. And it was precious not in the good sense–but precious because it shone light on the utter sanctity of life–on the value of each step we take towards a better job, a new partner, another horizon.

In this way, death, in an odd way, illuminates life even more, and makes us ponder and wonder and appreciate the small things–the cup of coffee at dawn, the kiss at dusk, and the love-making at midnight. Rashmi's death tore a dagger through my kidney, and tore us all apart, because she, of mostly all people, did not deserve to go to heaven at sixty.

The cancer that ate at her pancreas was cruel–it was monstrous–it was horrid–it was a storm that never stopped, a medical fiasco of heartbreaking proportions, and something that rotted at my then wife–a woman who is just as beautiful as she is weak to the ferocity of life's ills/cruelty. Keya and I were still so young when the cancer struck Rashmi, and we were just kids when we got married. Nothing about the situation was fair–not one bit made any sense, or could ever make any sense to begin with.

Rashmi's illness took a large chunk out of our marriage, and as newlyweds, we talked more about Sloan Kettering than we did of any honeymoon stateside or elsewhere. Some luxuries were not possible with Rashmi's cancer, and time was spent treating her body, and the declining state of her mind.

I don't think Keya and I were ready to take care of a sick parent–but then again, who is ever ready? There is no such thing as ready. People get sick, and some get unsick, and then others die. And therein lies the cruelty of life, but death–and I'll say this again–makes everything just so damn precious in the worst, most twisted, sordid way.

I'm a mess, Mom. Mess, mess, mess. I text Keya this at midnight, months after the divorce.

7

KEYA AND I kissed again. Her lips, as always, felt thin. I missed her touch.

She and I are still interconnected. Our breaths sync up sometimes—still—after all this time. Our heartbeats can be in alignment too. A part of her will never leave me. Her hair, her eyes, her skin will always remain in my body—tucked into my bones, present on my receding hairline. She's with me, at all times, even when I will be fifty, sixty, seventy, retired on a sailboat in the Mediterranean. Or in Annapolis, next to the sea. She will be there, even after I have been with many other women, and men, and more women at that. Keya will stay the same, living on the same Earth, walking on the same Earth, muttering platitudes to baristas and car washers on the same Earth.

She will be herself: her body, her mind, her spirit. Her heart. It will be there, and part of it next to me, when I'm on an Amtrak heading up the coast, in twenty years, her voice will sing to get off at Connecticut. At New Canaan, or New Haven. Her fingers will direct me in New York, past the Empire State, and through the Met, where she will point out Degas and Cezanne, and treat me to some Picasso as well.

I can't shake her touch. Her feel. Her security. She brought me back home, stable and sane. She fed me in the darkest of times.

She watched over my body as it writhed in bed, and sweated like a mad man during mania. Prolonged mania—mania not just for one week, or one month, but a full year, Mom. She saw the shirts full of manic sweat, when I would ring them out at 1, 2, 3 am, in the dead of night, when our demons were trying to lay to rest, to no avail, mine bigger than hers, or hers bigger than mine.

Indeed, I am going back to her tonight. To stay with her, just before she leaves for India. She's taking a bunch of stuff with her—some cashews to give to her uncle, some chocolate covered almonds for another relative. She'll arrive there—in Delhi or Hyderabad or Pune—and grace the subcontinent with her touch. Her singsong voice. Her body. The shop sellers and stall watchers and cab drivers over in that other country will be glad to meet her—happy to be in the presence of love. Of care. Just like I was, Mom.

Except now she is mostly gone. These nights I spend with her are seldom and fleeting—short visions of our past, when we curated more memories in front of Christmas trees and at Holi. Now Keya is a gift that is mostly away, unwrapped and out back together again and flung into the darkest waves of the Arabian Sea. Something is missing without her—missing more than just her name, her energy. Her spirit has been taken away from me and I don't know if it's ever going to come back.

I don't know if I'll ever find her in anyone else—in someone else—a woman or a man. Or any other gender in between. Her grace, her softness, her sensitivity to light and darkness is what propelled us together to begin with. Her love from all angles—from the top, from the side, out of thin air, her utter love, Mom.

Without Keya there is loneliness. Pure, uninhibited, unimpeded loneliness. Loneliness of the worst variety—the kind that makes the heart tangle into a complicated knot, then sink to the stomach. Loneliness that makes headaches even stronger, and pain harder to bear. Loneliness that pranks your body at night, making you think that someone will show up nearby, ready to hug you in the sheets. No one ever materializes, and it feels like no one ever will.

That's because Keya is gone. Gone with the wind, setting sail on a boat to India, seemingly never to come back again to my shores.

MY CLOSE FRIEND NEVER slept with Keya. That was all in my head. One big, fat cognitive distortion. It was a delusion. I'm delusional, Mom. You raised a delusional child. Everyone else in the family is in touch with reality—how did I become the odd one out? Can you explain this phenomenon? I need some sort of reason for why everything is fucked up.

Pain is around me everywhere I go. There's pain etched on the chest of drawers in my bedroom. Oma's picture is up there—she's smiling down at me, from heaven. Pain is in the air in this writing retreat—there is a pack of coyotes howling one hundred feet away. No one wants me in bed anymore. There's pain there.

One of these days the suffering will go away. The pain will disappear at death–I'll feel a jolt in my heart or my lungs might collapse, but then the madness will run away to the horizon, where it will bend past the sun, and over it, and then race to the moon, and watch me finally be at peace in heaven. Any traces of remaining insanity will ebb like the water does–in the Pacific–at the Puget Sound, where waves crash against Bainbridge, and that is the island where we were raised in America–several weeks or a few months each summer–and that is the only place that can give me peace, that can give me calm, that can seduce me with pebbled beaches and the looming skyline of Seattle, paired with the snow-capped mountaintops of Rainier. That is the island where Oma and Opa watched over us, and that is the island where I saw Opa die, but at least we were with each other, in the same house–the same enclave next to restless shores.

But besides Bainbridge–besides those childhood days–the pain will continue, the emotional pain will eat up my heart, the mania will slowly, day by day, week by week, and month by month, fry my brain, and the threat of psychosis will forever be ingrained, and I will never–and hopefully never–remember what happened during my first episode, although every bone in my body *wants* to remember, because it pains me to be a twenty nine year old young man–one with a healthy complexion, with sturdy muscles, and with enough testosterone flowing through my blood–well it pains me to be a young person and to have to admit to doctors that I don't remember a period of my life that could have lasted for days, weeks, or months. I want to know, desperately, what I looked like during the breakdown–if I didn't shower for days on end. I want to remember what kind of pants I wore, and which outfits I dressed in, and what I said. I want to remember which doctors I went to, and if I ever went to any kind of clinic. I want to know what thoughts were racing through my brain, and how many hours I slept, but I just don't know that–and I've never known–and I may never remember what happened, ever.

Usually, when I tell doctors I don't remember my first episode, they do a typical doctor thing of pretending not to be in shock, but small gestures on their face give it away–frozen eyes for a few seconds, a jaw that might drop a bit–just a tad bit–and sudden stillness across all of their body. And in that moment, I know they are scared–maybe scared of me, or scared of what happened, because they know that the turmoil I went through counts as a severe psychiatric issue, and they usually don't meet young patients who have amnesia over a certain event. Then they do another typical doctor thing, if they have good bedside manner, and they pretend like their body language just didn't give their utter fear away, and they move on to the next question–they might change their face a bit, or become more relaxed in their neck and torso, and their eyes will start moving again. They will ask me how many siblings I have, or what meds I'm taking. And then we move on to further topics, and we do a little doctor-patient dance, until we can't dance anymore–until they think they've figured me out and open the door, wave away, and then I wonder if they've ever had any other patients who didn't remember their first psychotic episode as well. And the answer is probably yes, but I want to meet these patients desperately, I want to scream into thin air for these friends to arrive and talk, but I can't scream, because the world would think I was crazy, and they would think those other people were crazy, and we'd just all be crazy together, but at least we would know the truth about this awful disease.

But the truth, most often, doesn't come out. Instead, we're left with prescriptions and therapists who make little jagged notes on paper, but we don't really understand what is going through our minds, and can't control it–and that lack of control is the scary part. The fact that this disease is still a mystery to many is frightening, and whatever turn it will take is scary, and *can* be scary, but somehow, I am not that scared, Mom–in fact, I am rarely scared of anything, mostly just myself. I'm scared of myself.

My hands are bloodied and there's no turning back. But men need to uphold their word.

DEATH IS TAUNTING AND it tastes good. A few bullets to the brain and it's all over–with a bang this time, and a little whimper. Most bipolar people want to kill themselves. It makes sense, really, given the savagery of the situation. Constant mania, meds for days on ends, endless doctors, and deep, deep, sinking depression. Add trans to that list and the world becomes worse: you are back in Hurt Capital, on the streets with heroin addicts and meth fiends.

I thought about death tonight. It's an easy way out–the purest way to get to heaven or hell. Only God will decide which dungeon I go to. Death is so enticing–so rapturing–so savory. I can't shake it off my shoulders.

They say that when you die, your life flashes by your eyes in just a few seconds. Those few seconds with you will be full of good things–negotiating with the Taliban, becoming ambassador, testifying in front of Congress. Those few seconds for me will be full of misery: car crashes and psychotic breaks from reality and embarrassing manic outbursts in college. And being teased and taunted because I wanted to be a man.

8

I SALIVATED AGAIN FROM the lithium. Foamy liquid came out of my mouth, drop by drop, at midnight–just before I was gonna go to bed. When this happens, my stomach also clenches into a knot, and becomes nauseous. Indeed, nausea fills my every crevice: every bone, every muscle, every mucous membrane wants to vomit. It's the worst feeling in the world–worse than fainting, worse than crying, worse than dying. I know I'm sick but refuse to be so: refuse because I'm only 29 and have 60 more years left in me. Or so I believe. I salivated for an entire hour. This meant that I got a stupid glass, and drooled in it, nonstop, for 60 minutes. I kept on turning and twisting, and twisting and turning, until the episode came to a halt. In my head, when I was writhing in bed, I thought of other 29-year-old men I knew who weren't unhealthy. Weren't trans. Weren't bipolar. These men probably go to bed at night knowing that they don't need a blood test the next morning, and they go to bed knowing that they can get in the pants of another woman with ease–convincing them of their stellar consulting job, their banking gig, their good DNA. Their gender–assigned at birth, perfect from the start. Unlike mine.

Doctors say that salivating is a bad thing, and I trust them on that. But I don't look into it too much–I don't surf the web, I don't go on Web MD. This time around, I will lie to my psychiatrist and say that it never happened. If I reveal the truth, he will cut my lithium dose to 300mg, and I can't afford to do that. My brain gets full of racing thoughts when I'm only on 300mg, and I turn into a maniac–a lunatic at every turn, when I have racing thoughts. It almost gets to the point where I want to kill myself, but that thought still evades me, and I won't put a Glock to my head, or tie a noose on the bedroom fan. I need 600mg of lithium to survive. So I'm going to lie, and lie some more, and if I salivate again–well, I'll twist and turn some more in bed and pretend like nothing happened. And I will writhe, and be nauseous, and be the sick man that you came to raise.

Let me describe what bipolar feels like in the head: it's like there's one hundred symphony orchestras playing all at once, except each orchestra is stringing a different tune: Beethoven, Bach, Mozart, but off beat–off kilter. Then the orchestras come to a grand finale and there's a series of percussion instruments that click and clang. And the drums go and then they keep going and keep going after that. Then thoughts of everyone around you start to crowd in the brain: an old professor who I had a crush on comes to mind, and I'm talking to her about literature. But then I think of Helen and her softball game today. And then I think of you. Back to the college professor. Now there's another symphony playing, and one of Drake's songs is on repeat. Then the traumatic memories start to crowd in: memories from college, and these memories make me sink to a bottomless trough–a place where despair rules and solace can't be found abound. Then I start pacing and pacing, walking to and fro, and crash on the bed because all of this noise is so loud–the intrusive thoughts are like AKs being shot, round after round, into the periphery. Into the distance. But now they're being shot into my head.

But even though I'm si–even though I'm sick–I can still deliver one thing to your doorstep, and that is the gift of writing beautifully. I will put some verbs down on paper, and I'll pair them with nouns unheard of, and I'll contort these words into a sentence that will blow you away. And that's what I'm mostly good for, Mom–I'm mostly good for my words. Everything else is a tossup, just like these lithium episodes.

There is a New York Times article from 2018. Dated July 28. *U.S. Diplomats Held Face-to-Face Talks with Taliban, Insurgents Say.* In it, they say that you talked to the Taliban. [name journalist here]

> *The talks took place in Doha, where the Taliban have long maintained an informal "political office" for the purpose of restarting the long-dormant peace process.*
>
> *They involved several members of the Taliban political commission and Alice Wells, the State Department's senior South Asia diplomat, as well as other unidentified American diplomats, according to the two Taliban officials.*

The Times posted a headshot of you, in the article, staring outwards. Your blue eyes are shining and your hair is coiffed into a shortcut. I wonder who the other men are. The men in the Taliban, the men from Afghanistan, the men trying to protect their version of a country. I wonder if you were scared during the meeting–perhaps, inevitably, always. I wonder if your hands were sweating. If your wrists were trembling. I wonder if you looked them in the eye–or if your chin darted to the right.

But most of all, I wonder what would have happened if the Taliban were my bipolar. If you were somehow negotiating with my bipolar at a table in Doha–a table otherwise meant for militants but now was cast as one with a disease. I wonder what you would have asked out of my bipolar–what you would have negotiated for.

First things first, I hope you would have asked them for less mania. Less hypomania, less excited curses at midnight, in my apartment, when all I want to do is jump on my bed or go for a glorious walk. I hope you would have asked for better nerves–for less social anxiety, more calmness when talking to others.

Second, I hope you would have asked for the best medicines, right off the bat. So I didn't have to experiment with Prozac, Zoloft, and Latuda. So I didn't have to dabble in Xanax or Ativan.

Lithium saved my life, Mama. It saved my fucking life.

THE STRESSES OF EVERYTHING–OF childhood, of teenage years, of the turbulence in college, of the hundreds of bouts of mania, and of the psychosis, make it seem like life will be short.

Everything about the disease seems unfair. It backtracks life a bit–making major milestones like college graduation and career goals delayed. Indeed, you might as well take two to five more years to accomplish every goal set in mind.

I salivated last night one more damn time from taking the godforsaken lithium. At one a.m. I got a sick feeling in my stomach, and saliva just started oozing out of my mouth. So I took a water bottle, emptied its contents into the sink, and started putting all of this goddamn excess saliva into this stupid water bottle. And my stomach was sick, and I was nauseous, and I hated the world when it happened.

I'm a si–I'm a sick son, Mama, and you raised a sick baby. You raised a kid that became sick as hell, and I will always be sick–I will goddamn *always* be sick, Mama. For the rest of time, for eternity, this sickness rots my bones, cripples my stomach, and erodes my intestines. It lives under my skin and makes me breathe in fear–fear that I can end up in the psych ward for the rest of my life–fear that I will go permanently crazy.

But Ma–but Mama–I am brill–I am brilliant beyond belief, and I swear and your mother's grave that that is the case, Mom. I swear that I am brilliant, and you see what I'm gonna do is this–here's what I'm gonna do–I will write so well, and so beautifully, that none of this will ever matter anymore, and the only thing that matters will be you reading the pages in this book, and other books at that.

Because I'm a literary genius, Mama. I'm a literary genius too. I *promise* you. I sure as hell am one. Stories of trans people suffocating at the helm of a cis torturer–stories of bipolar patients screaming at the top of their lungs–these stories will make do, for now, and they might even win some prizes.

Lit–litera–literature is what makes the world go round. The world thrives on good ass literature (GAL), good ass books (GAB), and good ass writing (GAW). All of these things are good–they are fine–and they sustain the creative energy ebbing and flowing on God's heavenly Earth.

The bipolar eats away at everything good–it is a monster that can't be controlled–a soldier gone rogue in Iraq, gunning at everyone–ISIS, Saddam Hussein, and Americans. The bipolar is a storm that takes over the poorest town in Kansas and sucks all of the houses away, past their pastures, and into the Midwestern night sky, where it devours people alive. The bipolar is a raging fire that takes over all of California and drowns celebrities in flames, drowns the Bay Bridge in flames, and drowns the Navy SEALs in San Diego in flames. The bipolar is God's way of putting you in premature hell–in a dungeon below the ground with Satan, except this time I'm standing *on* the ground–*on* Earth's soil–and still alive, rotting away in this horrible, awful, demonizing prison cell, trapped in between mania and psychosis, engulfed by depression, and on various highs and lows and booze benders throughout the day. The bipolar is my worst nightmare, it is evil, it is a cruel illness that only madmen suffer from.

I hate it with all of my heart–all of my twisted, brilliant mind.

And if you really wanna know the truth, Mama, I don't think I'm gonna live a long life. Not a long one at all. But I'm just trying not to die before you. That's why I live so *fast,* Mom. So goddamn fast all the damn time.

9

TONIGHT WE FOUGHT, Mom, and fought hard.

I explained that Dad has treated me differently since I became a man. He's reserved now, less soft around me–more of a hard ass. When I say *hey* to him he wants me to say *hi father* instead. I sense that he doesn't trust me–that he can't decipher me, that he doesn't understand my gender. He doesn't get what it's like to change from female to male, chick to a guy. It boggles his mind, and bogs him down in a way, placing him in an uncomfortable spotlight where he doesn't know how to talk and dance.

In a way, his treatment of me is gender affirming. Guy friends of mine have told me that their fathers aren't emotional with them–that they aren't sensitive, and don't have a sweet spot for them. Dad certainly has a sweet spot for Helen and Phoebe, and treats them like his little princesses. I am a prince gone rogue–a prince who needs to shower more, wake up earlier, and get better jobs, be they in private equity, banking, consulting, or government.

I'm not much of a bigger brother to Helen and Phoebe these days. Big brothers are supposed to look out for their other siblings–they're supposed to make lots of money and have their shit together. By the time big brothers in our family are 30, we're supposed to own a condo, and still be in the same marriage, and not get divorced, and have a stable job, with six figures, or, at the very least, own a company and be making more than that. Big brothers are supposed to be there so their sisters can call them if they ever need help–a lending hand–in case they need to fix the plumbing in their apartment, or fix their car, but I can't do *either* of those things, Mom, and big brothers are supposed to be an emotional shoulder to cry on, and I am barely that, because I am the one crying on other shoulders.

So I'm not so much of a big brother as a lost brother–a guy who has been lost in the shuffle, lost in change, lost in transition, lost in trans*lation*, lost in the utterly glorious, all-reckoning bipolar disorder. So sue me, Mama, if I can't be a big bro.

But as a brother, I will write so well that my lines will illuminate the finest of books, and these pages will be at Barnes and Noble, and they will sell well–sell heavily, sell heartily, Mom. And then I'll truly become a big brother, because then I can be strong, and be mighty, and be powerful, and people can come to my two shoulders to shed tears. That is the goal, after all–to have sturdy shoulders to cry on and a brain that isn't yet fried from hundreds of bouts of mania.

Indeed, mania has a way of frying the brain like a nice pan would to a sizzling egg–all cooked up with butter and a bit of oil and a yolk. The mania–well it just fries things, and it leaves things scattered, and very much not intact, and it leaves the mind racing, then racing some more, and then when those racing thoughts stop everything turns into a state of wholehearted confusion and disbelief.

When Dad is a hard ass around me, I retreat into my little writing shell–an enclave I build where I can sweep digital pages with the best verbiage and proper nouns around town. Mom, I might not be useful for anything in the aftermath of my mania, but I can give you a breed of writing that makes you see the finest literature in town. Indeed, if my writing *were* some sort of breed–a breed of dog–it would be the most expensive hound on the market–a pharaoh hound that swept prizes at Westminster. This hound would have the best fur, and the whitest teeth, and the best posture, and he would jump across obstacles with utter ease.

While Dad doesn't treat me like a sack of shit, he doesn't treat me like a pot of gold either, so I find myself navigating a middle ground with him: a pasture where I prove my worth through promotions and bonuses, bylines and timely chores. If Dad had a son at birth, I guarantee you that son would have wanted to be a CEO just like his father–a CEO with slick hair from costly cuts in DC, a CEO with manicured nails that are trimmed for meetings, a CEO with ties from Hermes and blazers from Brooks Brothers. That son would have been a wrestler, or a football player, and he would have had Dad's same posture–his same body–his same knack for women. The son would–perhaps like me–have gone to an Ivy school, or gotten a degree in business from Virginia Tech or UVA. The son would have been popular–a mild drinker at best, someone who knew how to summon the life of the party while only drinking three beers. The son wouldn't have gone to rehab. Wouldn't have been bipolar. Wouldn't have been manic for one year, writing strange poetry in the land of kooks.

I'm not this kind of CEO: I'm a vagabond at best, a prince–as I said–a prince gone rogue. I like listening to the Chili Peppers and smoking herbs now and then. I like publishing poetry books and talking about how to prevent suicide. Occasionally, I do like to suit up–this time in Jos A Banks–but that happens only on a full moon, when clouds don't shroud the night sky.

I am not meant to be Dad's son, Mom. I am not a guy who can fit into corporate culture. I can't schmooze my way to the top. I am not well enough to get a law degree, or an MBA. I can't waltz my way through trips to Riyadh and Doha and Istanbul. I can't go to Rwanda on short notice and sell missiles to foreign allies. I can't speak Russian at a consulate. I can't get invites to a Yudashkin fashion show. I can't do this, and I can't do that. But there is still a lot that I get done, in the shadows, in the background.

I believe I can win a Pulitzer one day. Or something close to it. I've been working on this fiction project–I've been working on this fiction project for a long time, and it's really good stuff. It's called King of DC, and I named it that because *I* am a king of DC, and the main character in the book is a guy just like me–a trans guy who grows up in the awning of Lincoln, Washington, and Jefferson–next to the Watergate and along the Potomac.

You said that I lie a lot. But how can I tell the truth if I don't know it myself? I do my best to discern right from wrong, truth from lie, but sometimes I just don't know what is best. If reality is distorted in my own head, then sometimes I will distort it to you. Tonight I'm going to go back to your place and show you all of my accounts. Stocks, bonds, Roths, my 401k, checking, savings. I'm going to come clean so you know I'm not lying about finances.

I'm at a standstill with you, Mom. If you don't trust me then how am I supposed to trust you?

Don't get me started on the morning I had a hallucination.

It was 2023. Just out of rehab and I was fired from that godawful job for being manic. Rashmi was dying of pancreatic cancer. In her last stages, she summoned hospice and was bedridden with a catheter and oxygen tanks for her lungs. In a dream, I envisioned a cluster of twenty something men–men with bulging torsos and toned legs. Men whose hearts are still beating properly. But one of them was dying as well, and he didn't know if he could make one more breath. I woke up in shock, and I saw a black spider barreling at me. I also hear police sirens. The spider is black, and fuzzy, and has too many legs to count. Petrified, I tried to bat it away from the bed. My hands were shaking and shaking on linen, then shook in the air. But no spider materialized, Mom. I didn't bat anything away. My hands didn't feel any spider flesh, any spider arms, any spider eyes or organs. Instead, the spider disappeared out of thin air–just like that–and left me alone. And what's more, there were no cops around. No police cars to make any noise. The hallucination left me writhing. That's life, Mama. Life is scary. And it is brutish, and short, just like what Hobbes said. Life is hard. Just like the one that had been taken from Rashmi.

I don't think I'm meant for this life, Mom. I was just born so *different.* So strange. But they say the best literary minds hail from strange people and I–I–I deliver literary excellence on a silver plate to your dinner table. On the plate, there are the initials of my favorite authors–EH for Hemingway, TM for Toni Morrison. There are also some of my favorite words–*smorgasbord, literati, divine.* This smorgasbord of words will launch me into the divine class of the literati.

I am a broken man. I got drinks a while ago with a member of the CIA–he was in their Directorate of Operations. We were at one of those joints, nestled in a suburb of northern Virginia, where spooks and consultants live side by side. I met him off of Grindr, and he, after a few beers, told me that he used a gun at work. All in all, he wasn't the best guy around. Would cut me off after saying a few words. Would interrupt like none other. Had a bald head, and strong physique. He said that he had met many trans people. That he slept primarily with trans women, mainly because he wanted to be one himself. He thought most trans people seemed broken inside, but not me. He told me that I wasn't broken. Now I beg to differ. With rehab, with Rashmi's death, with the booze and the benzos, I think God has left a few tears on my heart. But he can't tear the whole thing entirely.

The first church I worship is one of alcohol, and the second church is one of literature. Specifically, literary excellence. I belong to the *literati*–a class of divine writers speaking the truth through one off adverbs and verbs that cut straight to your head. Writing is not a hobby, it's not a passion, and it's not a job. It's a spiritual practice, and it is its own church. It is a form of healing, and it keeps me alive during the day, and at night, on Dad's farm, when howling dogs and sick beavers scream past water and trees alike. Writing protects me, Mom. If you and Dad can't do that, then literature will. I have the Gift of Gab. I have a way with words.

There is nothing more divine than the way *literati* spells itself across a piece of paper. There is nothing more divine than an m-dash after one clause, to be followed by a trio of details in the next. I believe in a Rule of Three–I believe that piecing three words together with commas is just as divine as composing an entire book. I believe words work well in threes. I believe that adverbs should be cut at all costs. I believe that young children and teenagers and twenty somethings living in abject poverty can use, at their very best, the written word to etch themselves out of dire straits.

I believe that many writers want to kill themselves, but not me. I've never taken a gun to my head, Mom. I've never swallowed too many sleeping pills. My lack of suicidality shocks therapists and psychiatrists, when I'm sitting on their plush couches next to a box of Kleenex. These days, I never get depressed to the point where I want to take my own life. My depression is mild at best: I'm either miserable from the lithium or just plain done with people around me. If my landlord yells, or if my boss is nasty, then I fall into a spiral of despair. But not the kind of despair that would summon a noose to the neck.

I believe life is precious. As a transman with bipolar, the chances I would have wanted to die are quite high. According to the National Institute of Health, between 25% and 60% of bipolar patients will attempt suicide at least once in their life and one fifth (around 20%) will have completed suicide.

The suicide rate for trans people hovers at around 50%.

Taking into account the formula for the probability of two cumulative events, the chances that I will have completed suicide hovers at around 30%. And that doesn't take into account the repetitive nature of suicidality. Many trans people with bipolar want to take their life every day of the week. If their chances of taking their life are around 30% each day, the chances they will go through with it are still very high.

Yet suicide evades me. Some way, somehow. It runs away from me. It's scared of me. I'm fighting back, and it won't win. It never will. I believe too much in life for the chance of death to ever take over.

I won't perish by suicide, and refuse to let any suicidal feelings get the best of me, too. I contemplate, often, whether life is worth living, especially as someone who is a fetish–someone who can never fit into the crowd. But life is, indeed, worth living–with the extra addendum to live out miserable times by cocooning in a hollow of books, fictional worlds, and favorite authors.

Literature is redemption, Mom.

The world of books and letters is the best one to exist. The world of the Literati–of one where literature thrives–is a world where people learn from mistakes and don't repeat old ones. Students can learn the travesties of history through literature, and teachers can profess to them as well. Being apart of literature means being apart of a movement greater than the self: one in which plots are thicker than the day's heat, where characters roam free without rule, and where settings can be magical lands curated for the senses to bear.

What's rather unsettling is that the best books are those that make others uncomfortable–ones that make you squirm in your seat on the Metro North train, ones that make you howl for some sort of normalcy at the break of dawn–past five beers–past two whiskey shots–when one is drunk, inebriated, intoxicated to words. The best works of art rattle the mind and make us, strangely, twistedly, sadly, wanting for more, even though the art that just fed us was disturbing at its core.

The best literature is meant to comfort the disturbed and disturb the comforted. Remember that, Mom. Raskolnikov, from *Crime and Punishment,* was crazy–a deranged Russian man sentenced to the gulags. Gregor Samsa, from *The Metamorphosis,* was deeply troubled at heart, and Kafka made a point to show that. And he showed it damn well. Even Voldemort is obviously troubled. Putting JK Rowling's bigoted antics aside, her evil character was frightening. Dementors sucked the souls out of Hogwartsians, just as words should suck the soul out of readers. In *Beloved,* Toni Morrison writes of a mother who kills her two year old so she doesn't have to be born into slavery. I don't know what's more disturbing than *that,* Mom. But it's disturbing for a purpose–for a glorious reason–to make us thrive on being disgusted and repulsed by stories. Stories should shake us, they should make us tremble, they should leave us gasping for air, for our life, so we can breathe again–breathe freely, knowing that we just learned a good lesson.

This is literature, Mom. And it is nothing more–nor nothing less–than that: discomfort. Raw, undogged, unfettered discomfort, shining through letter after letter, page after page, tortured author after tortured author.

10

I TRUST THAT SOMEDAY all of your light will seep through me and illuminate the parts of me that need to heal. I need to heal desperately: a sinking worm gasping for water. A beaver craving a dam. A hawk in search of prey.

Your nebula, shining bright in a country black sky, guiding me to better days. Days where I don't have to take lithium. Days where I don't see spiders out of thin air. Days when I don't hear police sirens.

When your light shines through, the bipolar will fade away. It will disappear into the horizon to never come back. It will crumble to sordid pieces and rot like old bread in a compost bin. It will die in a flame I curated through doctors appointments and last minute pills. It will go away, never to be seen again. Never to reappear again. Never to attack my brain again.

When this happens, I'll be on Top of the World. I'll become an investment banker and make two million a year. I'll get an MBA at Harvard. I'll travel to Tahiti and meet the woman of my dreams. I'll propose to her in Paris, in the heart of the Louvre, and I'll wed her in the south of France, near Tropez, at Club Monaco. I'll never think about depression again. Never think about mania. Never think about suicide.

THE BIPOLAR MAKES ME sensitive to everything: every twig rustling in the leaves, every dog barking at midnight, every odd stare from a gentleman on the street. The slightest chaos can rupture my eyes and ears and give me illusions of reality: fake images and sounds to crowd my brain. When this happens, I put the world on hold. Earth's heart stops to beat for a second. And what a tiny, ruptured second it is. But then the world moves again: trains are on time in New York, I drive to Queens and eat samosas in Jackson Heights. I kiss a woman again. And then a guy. And then *another* woman. And then I read some Kant, and some Toni–some Toni Morr–Toni Morrison–my favorite of all time. The best to have ever lived. A woman who outshone Shakespeare, Hemingway, and Camus, all at once.

I really don't wanna be sick Mama–I really don't wanna be sick. But you gave birth to a sick son. I was sick starting at seventeen. I have to be strong for Helen and Phoebe. But I'm simply not, Mom, I'm simply not–but I am a literary ge–I am a literary genius Mama, I can promise you that. I can promise that to Helen and Phoebe and Dad as well, and damn near any person who crosses my way. I can string words together like none other, Mom, and I'll string some words together for you, so you can love me some more, and so that I can become just a bit stronger so Helen and Phoebe can feel secure in their older brother.

But I am far from an older brother right now, Mom, because the bipolar is eating away at my brain and rotting me alive, it is sledgehammering me into a trough of the worst war time dirt, and it is rusting my soul. The bipolar might be doing me in for good right now, and there might be no turning ba–no turning back from here. But I'm going to promise you one thing, and I'm going to promise it again: I'm gonna write, Mama, I'm going to write my way out of hell, I'm going to write my way into the horizon, where stars shine and the moon sleeps happy next to Orion and the Big Dipper. I'm going to write so strongly that some people in France and the UK will know my name, and I'm going to write so eloquently that professors past Ivy gates will speak of my lines.

Literature is what makes the world go round, and I am going to etch my name into the literary canon so those around me don't have to suffer anymore. I'm going to write about trans men who haven't made it yet, but I'm going to write so that they *can* one day make it in life, and I'm going to write so heroin addicts don't have to use the needle again, and hell–I'm going to write erotica that will make suburban housewives fall in love with me.

Once I'm done writing, the bipolar will go away, just like that–*poof*–and the disease will be cured. The finest adjectives on the market will take away the mania, and the best verbs in the universe will cure depression. And the most pointed nouns–both proper and common–will ease anxiety, and put together–when all of these things are put together–the psychosis will go away, just like that. Just like that, Mama. And I won't have to suffer again–I will never have to suffer a single time, ever again. Life will be made of rainbows and butterflies and golden chocolates. Neighbors won't make fun of me and friends won't stab me in the back. Hurt Capital won't exist–it will be a city sequestered for others–others who have sinned or who haven't figured out their suffering yet.

This is the way of the world, Mom–to write, and write beautifully at that.

I RUN AWAY TO a place where there are no problems: where the sun shines freely without being told to. Where the Earth can rotate all day long, and rays still hit your face at the speed of light. Strangely, this place in my mind is often back in Russia, not in Moscow or St. Petersburg, but in one of the ring cities, at a monastery, in the dead of winter. It is a Russian winter, Mom, the cruelest kind–the worst season to fear. Fear above all else. A winter that will suck your soul, leave your skin crumpled and withering, transform you into a pale ghost. In this ring city, it is dark, it is grim, but you and I are sitting near a fireplace recounting the icons we just saw. We're talking in Russian, Mom–Russkiy. Gavarit parusskу again. And we're just shooting the shit, you and I, until the day is done with. Until we can get a cup of tea and retire for the night. In these days, the bipolar doesn't exist, and I am neither trans, nor cis–just a human being. Without a gender. And you're not gendered as well. No one, in fact, is gendered. Not even the icons. Not even the nuns.

In another world, you and I are also sitting on Bainbridge Island–just on the cusp of the Puget Sound, near Seattle. This is where you grew up. We're watching two ferries pass by each other on the water, and Oma and Opa are alive again. Oma is telling a story about Germany, and Opa is cursing everyone out. One of us is mad at Opa, but we let the anger slide, and listen to a tale of the Black Forest and Hitler's hegemony. The waters of the Puget are calm with slight waves, rustling currents and orcas dwelling under the oncoming tide. Mount Rainier is in the distance, and its iced tiers poke out of the sky–faces of cliffs looming over the islands.

In a third pretend world, Helen and I are on a flight overseas, to Colombia–to Cartagena. We've already been there, and we'll go there again. We're at the airport terminal in Bogota, changing flights, and three hours later we arrive alongside a beautiful coast with Portuguese architecture and the Caribbean Sea. Gabriel Garcia Marquez's house is on the water, and I walk by it, hoping I can push out books like he did some day. Helen and I get coffee on the sands and don't think about the past–in fact, we treat the past as a present that was, but now we've torn its wrapping paper and shredded it into the sky. The only thing that matters, in Cartagena, is what is on the edge of the horizon–the new futures we can glean from good conversation and laughter–conversation about our goals and dreams for what *can* be and not what *has* been. What *has* been is a rotten amalgamation of memories–manic episodes I am ashamed of, when I lunged at arbitrary people and spent thousands on purchases, got a sullen tattoo of Milkman on my left bicep and ran away to New York City, bordering on psychotic, to stay in a hostel with *hostile* foe. That is what *has* been. But what *can* be is a smoldering of achievements in years to come–books written, prizes won, crosswords completed, vacations done, girls bagged, beaches swam, jobs to be had. Paychecks made every two weeks, and more conversation and laughter with Helen, in another world city.

This conversation is what will sustain us for years to come–and as I sai—as I said–I need to make more conversation with others, in cities near and far, to mend broken ties. These conversations will be the hardest to bear, but the most fruitful in the long run. Until I can have these talks, I remain a tortured soul.

Before I was hearing cop sirens and seeing spiders that weren't real there was a world I inhabited that was free of turmoil. This world was called childhood, and it was a kingdom you brought to us, full of endless ice cream scoops and maniacal kicking and screaming in pools and soccer games. In this special kingdom, the world was a playground and our oyster, rife with swing dances in Virginia and mehndi in India. There was no rape back then–no gender bending–no violence, or very little violence, and little death too. Instead, life was simple. A slice of apple pie to be devoured after dinner. A piece of the best lemon meringue after a long day of playing in the sands. Britney Spears was on full blast, and Justin Timberlake was still a member of the Disney Club. Then NSYNC came into fruition, and the Backstreet Boys, and suddenly Aaron Carter was playing basketball with Shaq.

You were the best ambassador in the business. Your hair shone blonde, your eyes blue. You boarded helicopters with four stars. Saw AKs in real life. Met SEALs and Delta Force.

I'm afraid you've given birth to a daughter turned son who is potentially sick in the head and incapable of doing things. Of boarding planes, just like you, to Kenya and Istanbul and Pakistan. Of writing memos to Clinton and Trump. Of meeting with the Taliban in Doha.

I'll say bye to bipolar, Mom, forever. I promise you that.

11

THE PILLS IN the bathroom cabinet are painters now. Rothko is making an entire canvas red, and then making another one teal and yellow. Picasso is taking noses and legs and arms and bending them into every which way, then placing them next to circles and triangles, all aglow in violet and lavender and burgundy and orange. Monet is making the best impressionist painting on the market–there are white lilies in Paris, floating on a river, and Da Vinci is still the patron child of the Medicis. The Mona Lisa is shining high and bright at the Louvre, and thousands of tourists are lined up to see her that day in the first arrondissement.

These works of art will bring me back to life, and quell all that is remaining of the bipolar. The bipolar, actually, will be made gone forever because of the painters–these glorious painters, Mom. The mania will subside into the upper echelons of the atmosphere, and skyrocket themselves past a Boeing and into the stratosphere, next to Orion and all of the other stars. And the painters will make sure that I'll never be psychotic again–not one bit–so that I can have a happier life moving forward–and really, when it comes down to it, the painters might even erase the possibility of ever having to take a pill again. But that day still has to come.

HURT CAPITAL

I've started watching Jason Bourne to feel like I have a friend.

In these movies, Bourne–an ex-CIA assassin–traces his former kills–one that he's forgotten, just like I've forgotten moments as well. After running on the beach in Goa, Bourne starts to have flashbacks through dreams, just like I might have some flashbacks through dreams as well.

I don't remember my first psychotic episode. I tell my doctors I don't remember it. It could have lasted for days, weeks, or a couple of months. I wouldn't know the difference. Helen says that I thought you were going to kill me. I wonder what I did in those moments–if I made a bomb shelter or a gate around my room. I wonder if I kept a knife in a drawer. I wonder how I thought you were going to kill me–if I thought you had a pistol the State Department lent you, if I thought you copped a bomb from Gaza or an IED from Baghdad. Helen says that I also didn't shower for days on end. I wonder what I smelled like–if my hair was as greatest as the Exxon oil you sell to foreign countries, if it slicked back into curves. I wonder if there was a buildup or dirt under my nails, if my clothes were browning, if my room became a cesspool of odor. I wonder what I said during the episode. If I screamed at the top of my lungs, or if I heard any voices. I wouldn't know. My brain has taken that time and thrown it back into the recesses of my memory, gone to a trash can I can't take the lid off of.

Bourne is the only guy I feel I have anything in common with.

I have known men who live in the darkest of places–in capitals more hurt than mine. These men have raped and pillaged, and done inextricable harm to others. They have stolen and been thieves. They have gone to jail.

I cannot properly describe what a psychotic episode feels like. The inner rungs of your brain stop to work, becoming a jumble instead. Neural synapses start firing to the wrong other synapses, or stop firing altogether. Dopamine gets released in the wrong places, or not released at all. Serotonin says goodbye.

Slowly—just bit by bit—the work doesn't make sense anymore. Things around you become unreal, and then real again, and then back to unreal. You board a plane in Cleveland and think that the plane is going to kill you in some way—that its turbines somehow only hate Isabel, and Isabel Amend. That the plane's engine will reach out a helping hand to strangle your throat.

Then you think that people around you are having abortions—that these women you knew got Plan B and it failed. Just somehow failed. You think, without any conversation, that the sweeper on the street belongs to a cult, because his left sleeve is rolled back in a certain way that suggests so. You think that a professor in class is cancerous even when they are not. You are deeply, deeply unwell, Mom.

During a psychotic episode, at night you briefly have the capacity to wonder if the world will somehow turn into a better place for you the next day—if, indeed, people will start to treat you better, like you are one of them, like you are not sick and instead a ray of heaping sunshine. You wonder if things in your head will get better—if they'll improve in any way—if your body will be more toned, if doing a crossword while crazed will somehow make the tentacles in your brain less wildly loose and more put together.

With medicine, this dream is capable of happening. The proper antipsychotics will but the head at rest again and make synapses less loose—less destructive. Day by day, you'll learn that that Boeing 767 didn't, indeed, want to kill you, and that its turbines merely wanted to take you back to Reagan Airport, safe and sound, with a bag of salted United peanuts to accompany. You'll learn that the professor you thought was somehow dying really is not, and will be teaching for semesters to come. You'll learn that the woman you thought was having an abortion—for no reason whatsoever—is actually celibate. You'll learn that the street sweeper is not actually part of a cult but is a Catholic who practices his religion now and then, but not feverishly.

When these thoughts start to become corrected, you will finally like being on the planet—planet Earth again. You will enjoy the hot feel of a coffee against your palm and the writhing waves of the Atlantic, at a beach in North Carolina or Jersey. You'll actually like the feel of a roller coaster ride at Coney Island and the thrill of the eye of a hurricane in Florida. These things, above all, will appear real again, and that's God's greatest gift—to finally offer you something that makes sense.

Jason Bourne is on a fact finding mission to learn the truth. And I'm on a fact finding mission to learn the truth as well, Mom. One day, I will have all of the facts of my past–every single nugget of my history. And everything will be illuminated, and things will finally make sense for once in this goddamn lifetime. Because right now, well I have amnesia right now, and I don't know everything that has happened to me, Mom. And I don't know everything *about* me. And it doesn't hurt as much as it leaves a vacancy in my heart that could be filled with preciousness–with a feeling of camaraderie to memories past–with a feeling of knowing and being cognizant and being aware and fully feeling what is right to feel given the conditions. But until that day passes, I will remain like Jason Bourne.

THE YEAR OF MANIA was amazing, and I miss it with every fiber in my body–every bone in my leg and arm. I can't even begin to describe what mania feels like, at its peak, when elation and jubilation take hold, and the precipice of something new–a new horizon–a new confidence–appears out of thin air.

Imagine the best kind of high–better than heroin, better than cocaine, better than California's finest weed, and better than the most expensive bottle of Scotch on the market. Actually, imagine being a junkie and doing all of those substances at the same time. Or imagine being a foodie, and eating at fifty Michelin starred restaurants in the span of sixty days. Then imagine being a loser–being a downtrodden outcast at school–a social pariah–a boy who was spat on and kicked in the dirt, and imagine the homecoming queen asking him out on a date. Now imagine this: imagine you are a ne'er-do-well constantly bordering on a state of homelessness, only to find that you won the ten million dollar lottery at the grungy 7-Eleven next door. Suddenly, you buy a mega mansion in Miami and even purchase a luxury sailboat while you're at it. You teach yourself to sail, and go to bed with the finest-looking Russian model, and eat caviar at midnight, and down Dom Perignon at one. And this ne'er-do-well never has to worry about money again–never.

Bipolar is the sickest of mental diseases, because it creates a fake happy feeling and convinces you that it is real–that it is good–only to find out that this shell of an emotion is slowly destroying your brain–frying it and potentially causing hallucinations, tremors, night sweats, racing thoughts, and more. Bipolar essentially works to prop up the illusion of confidence through mania–and patients believe this confidence–we think it is real, we think it is good for us, and we want it to stay.

What's more, after we have been told by doctors to treat the confidence, we crash, and the mania fades, and what is left is a sweeping, grand, dark depression–the worst kind of depression to bear–a cloud so gray–so ugly–that it looms above our heads, like that storm I just talked about, and this cloud of sadness is not made better by alcohol, it is not made better by anything, and it takes months to clean it up–if it ever gets cleaned up after all.

Bipolar is twisted–it is a twisted disease–it is a horrific illness, it messes with the mind and takes dopamine away, crushing it into a bottomless garbage bin. Bipolar plays tricks with our minds, it deceives us, it makes us think that the happiness it gives us is beneficial in any which way. The jubilation through mania that bipolar offers can kill someone quicker, putting them in a state of cognitive decline in rapid succession. Preventing this decline is the key to attacking the illness.

The bipolar is one looming, giant storm over a person's head, Mom. It makes the world around us indecipherable–and utterly chaotic. Things that are supposed to make sense end up being a puzzle. It's hard to read people sometimes: their feelings, their thoughts, their intentions. We pray that all the sounds we hear are real, and all the things we see are real too. I pray that my understanding of the environment around me is closer to the truth than it is to some false delusion, but I have no way of knowing what is going on. Instead, I spend my days hoping that what I think is more right than wrong, and hoping that the actions I take will make more progress than backward steps.

The mind is never satisfied, never, Mama.

12

THERE IS AN east Asian girl in my life who wants to have sex with me, really badly. Women annoy me these days. They're too judgmental–too picky about what men should do. It's the judgment that really gets to me. They judge everything–what brand shoe you buy, what t-shirt you wear, what meal you eat for lunch (whether it's tofu salad or McDonald's), what you say (what comes out of your mouth), which sex position you prefer, what your career trajectory is.

Women look at bad behavior as flawed, not realizing that everyone can fuck up. They're irritating. Some women are better than others–not casting any judgment on anyone.

I am at the strip club again. I know I probably shouldn't tell you about these kinds of things, but Keya ratted on me at the end of our marriage and wel–well–you found out.

I am not interested in these women at all. Their bodies don't mean a thing to me. But the lights do. The flashing incandescent bulbs, the raging rap music over the stereo–California Love by Tupac is my favorite. The feel of white cloth on the table–dirtied from past customers. Perhaps some sleazy.

I love the metal detector that the bodyguard waves around my body. It feels as if I'm about to board a flight to the Green Zone, in Baghdad, or to Kabul–where you've negotiated with terrorists. It feels like I may be packing heat myself, and I might be packing heat in another country–maybe Israel, where I flirted with death at an empty fish market in Jaffa, or maybe Islamabad, where we were evacuated from the embassy due to the threat of war. Or maybe I could pack heat in Cyprus, where I was hit by that damn car.

Bad Bunny is playing now, and my favorite stripper is on the pole. Her name is Carly. She has blonde hair and is from LA. She comes over to hug me, smoothly, after, because we are friends. At least friends in the club. Another dancer comes up to me and gives me her Instagram–they both know I won't hurt them, won't touch them. I'm harmless, soft, sensitive, and an ally.

I go here also because it reminds me of danger and risk–the kind of risk that I felt in Moscow when Helen and I snuck out of the compound, past waking hours and to the Arbat, where I could pound my body relentlessly with alcohol and cigarettes. Or to Rosinka, where I would make out with a girl or stupid guy.

And I'd go back to my room, and feel the wrath of smoke take over my lungs, and it would remind me how the wrath of gender was taking over my body, as my bones and skin secretly yearned to be a man, but knew that I couldn't, because Russia is as transphobic as snow is white on a Hallmark Christmas Card.

So going to this strip club, where I can envision being raped or robbed in the men's bathroom, with sleazy men, reminds me of the danger of my childhood, and I can't get away. I just can't, Mom. The strippers are merely props to pay and look at–but nothing else. The danger is what I seek.

To be trans is an act of rebellion, but it is also an act of servitude. To transition genders means to change to be a better person–a refined man–but this also means placing yourself as a slave in modern day America. Being trans means committing yourself to being a second class citizen. Once the transition is done, the second class citizenry will stay with you for the rest of your life. People often ask me if I'm happier now that I'm a man. The short answer is yes, but the longer answer is both yes and no.

It's a lonely road to find yourself. It entails putting oneself into the unknown–in cities untraversed and mountains still loose with fire. Finding yourself means kissing the wrong woman. Or man. It means breaking a vodka bottle on cobblestone to see the way the shards fall out of one piece. It means running for miles only to catch a sunset that is already half gone, with orange and red hues pranking the eye. It means putting your hand through one thousand sand grains and catching nothing but the remnants of a dirty shell. It means listening to the same song for hours on end, expecting a different result. This is the definition of insanity.

Finding yourself means getting into the lives of the wrong people–of thugs and gangsters and murderers who want to snatch your soul. It means being at gunshot, your head just feet away from a rifle. It means coming home to an empty bed for more than three hundred days in a year, and more days after that. The people who *should* be in the bed are gone missing–or out on town making their spirits alive with burning tequila. These people *could* be my lovers but aren't. They're missing out on my heart, unbeknownst to them–they're missing every beating artery, full of love and trepidation.

Society feels different now–society feels like a bully pit, and not a welcoming wonderland of friendly faces and intimate relationships. Suddenly, everything becomes tense: walking into a bathroom late at night, at a club, and wondering if the man at the sink will stab me if he saw my actual genitalia. When women and men hit on me at this club, I also wonder if they will punch me, slap me, or insult me if I tell them I'm trans. In the workplace, I don't disclose my gender identity at all, instead just choosing to pass. But then people inevitably find out, and social interactions become different if they are transphobic.

Trans guys don't get a lot of love in this world, Mama. We just don't. The lesbians barely like us because they think we're icky—dying too hard to be masculine. They want female curves and soft lips. The straight men don't like us because they think we're losers—maybe too short, too high pitched, or even competition to them, at our best. The gay men don't like us because they don't like our private parts, and might just think that we're butch lesbians. And what's more, *we* don't like each other because we're all competing against each other to begin with. So the world is a cruel, cruel place, Mom. And that's just the half of it.

They said that because I wanted to become a man that they wouldn't love me. Wouldn't touch me. Wouldn't kiss or hug me. Wouldn't want to date me at *all*, Mom. And I just couldn't stand it, Mama. I went back to my car that night and just writhed to and fro in the passenger seat—just like that—twisting back and forth.

It's hard for trans people to find love, Mom. Despite the beauty you gave me—despite my beautiful face—which takes just after yours—I have a hard time finding love. We can first start with how society treats us. Sixty percent of Americans still think that gender is defined by the sex we were assigned at birth. Forty-two percent of transgender adults have tried to take out life because of how shitty the outside world looks at us. Then move on to dating. Dating as a trans man, even in today's America, and in today's Washington DC, is excruciatingly difficult. Let's start with some numbers, Mom. Let's say that 5% of women in DC are truly queer. And I lo—I love queer women Mom—I think they make the world go round. In fact, I only want to date queer women, and not men. Because most people think I'm a gay man, and I also look young, let's reduce the number of queer women who would date me by 1%. I'm being generous here. It could be more than 1%. And let's just say that not all queer women would sleep with a transman. Let's say that, shall we, 40% of queer women would. That would make the percentage of women attracted to me in DC hover around 1.6%. So if I lined up on a street, and saw one hundred beautiful, intelligent women in Washington DC, only around one or two of them would consider sleeping with me.

Now let's move on to men. Dating men. Now most people think I'm gay, but I'm really not—I'm quite bisexual. I love men and women equally and in fact, during the height of my love season, I love women far more than I love men. Men are awful. They are the scum of the Earth. They are pond scum, to be precise. Just like that red-haired Ohioan who slept with Keya. Men hate me. They hate trans people. They have subjected us to violence in the past—men, indeed, kill trans women and other trans men. Men are the reason why the Earth cannot be flat. Why the sun has to inevitably set. Men start wars and killed my rabbit in India. I named him Bush Bush after the president only to realize he was a man who started the worst war of them all. Men seize oil from fiefdoms and rape widows. Men make widows. Men rape bachelorettes and girls and talibs. Men cave to desire. Men desire what they cannot have. Men sometimes have what they can't sell—a child in suburbia who plays lacrosse and was a Boy Scout. Men scout clubs for women who look weak. Men are weakened by morning wood and a tremble in between their thighs. Men tremble at women making better pay.

I will make men pay for their crimes, one day.

I hate men. Hate, loathe, despise, Mom. They are the bane of my existence. The only use they serve is conversation over beer at a sport's bar. The only joy I get out of men is poker night with the other lads. The only men I like are ones who have been to jail or sacrificed their bodies and minds in other ways: men with tattoos, men with some piercings, men with mug shots. Men who have seen the worst of the Earth and still choose to come back. Men can sympathize with my struggle. Men who are okay with my manic nights, with wringing the sweat out of my second t-shirt at 4am. Men who appreciate my body—who don't hate my scars and my vagina. Men who can still call me a man afterward.

Most men who I used to sleep with are still good to me. Maybe that is a product of being raised in DC—and of being surrounded by men who also hate Trump. At this writing retreat, I am texting one of my ex-boyfriends from high school. I had many, you know, Mom. Many ex-boyfriends. His name is Andrew, and he is kind to me. Now in Vermont, he was visiting DC again and wanted to get a drink. But his Mom shared news of cancer just one day prior to him coming here. So we held off on drinks for now. But, in a fit of despair, I texted him about my career, or rather, lack thereof.

The world is cruel, and it tells me–and others–that we are less desirable, less lovable, less okay as people. It's hard not to internalize these thoughts–to digest them one by one, and let them feed our personality. Many others are repulsed by our bodies, or at least find them nominally repulsive, but would sleep with us if no one found out. This is one of the biggest cruelties of them all: men and women wanting to feast on our bodies but lying about that to everyone's faces, because they are so ashamed of their own desire for us. Now *that* is truly repulsive.

MOM, I'M A CREATIVE and literary genius. I've told you that before, and I'll tell you again. But during tonight's in person conversation I *told* you that I was a creative genius, and you told me not to tell anyone. To be silent about it. Quiet as a hawk seeking prey. The truth is that the world operates in waves and energetic circles: the sunrises around me are reminders to stay in tune with Earth's godly flow and the sunsets are just notifications to go to sleep happy.

Except I'm still in Hurt Capital. I posted on lesbian Reddit and asked all of the lesbians if the world what they thought of trans men. I asked if they would ever *date* a trans man. Ever fall in *love* with one. Ever want to be *intimate* with us and all of that jazz. And do you know what the lesbians of the world had to say, Mama?

I've never really understood female sexuality. I've never understood what makes one lesbian attracted to both women and trans men and what makes others not. I don't know how lesbians choose to like each other. I don't consider my*self* a lesbian, Mama. Not anymore.

There must be *some* lesbian who wants to date me—*someone* out there must still care, Mom. These lesbians just told me to date bisexual and straight girls, which *does* make sense, until it doesn't. Until I've found that the odd lesbian in my past life actually did have a crush on me after all of these years. And there's no explaining that, Mama.

I've spent most of my twenties in empty bars and on broken tables. When I wasn't married to Keya, most of my life was alone. At these bars. Next to beer and shots of tequila. And endless glasses of wine, praising my second church of alcohol. Booze is what makes the world go round, Mom. But it won't go round too much. It won't spin around too much for me. Just a little—just enough to get tipsy and happy.

Last night, I went to a bar and a guy saw my old credit card. He saw Isabel spelled on it. He figured out I was a *tranny* and even called me one. He called me a fucking tranny, Mom. Then after that, he compared me to a porn star. He said that I either worked in the porn industry or was a sack of lies. I told him the opposite. I said that I've owned a company in the past, and that it was really successful. That I made a lot of money doing it. He said he didn't believe me. That because I am a tranny I can't operate a good business and make any profits. He said that trannies don't do that. Not around here, anyways.

I almost fought back. Almost took my hand and threw it into his left jaw. Into his front teeth. His forehead. His cheeks. I wish I did, Mama. But I wouldn't have been able to resist his punches. I'm not sure if the bartender would have had my back either.

Do you want to know what else happened? This man got my Instagram. He tried to friend me on the platform, to see what more I was made of. He's a sick and twisted monster, Mom. I messaged him telling him he could fuck off. Fuck off into the horizon—into the Alps, into the Arctic sea, into the plain buttes of Kansas. Fuck off until I didn't see him anymore, Mama.

The world is run by monsters. Dominic Strauss Khan, head of the IMF, was sleeping with prostitutes in French hotel rooms. Vladimir Putin is unhinged right now—he used to not be this violent when we were in Moscow. John F Kennedy asked for hundreds of sexual favors in the White House pool. Bill Clinton has raped women. Hillary Clinton has lied about it. Trump is a demagogue turned villain.

The world is a deeply troubling place. Rendering words to recount how troubled it indeed is is the best part of the day. Many fathers out there have raped women in the past—but usually not their wives. Many bosses in restaurant kitchens ask for sexual favors from waitresses in exchange for some loose change. These waitresses are done with, taken advantage of, thrown into the dust. Some young people fall ill to diseases that only shake the elderly. Yet they get sick and die far too early for anyone's own good. See what I'm saying: the world is a troubled place. Weapons companies make hundreds of millions selling missiles to pour down on Yemen. Rogue arms dealers prance around Peru and Russia trading noxious chemicals for Chinese yen. Women manipulate others so they feel worse about their bodies. Alcoholics choose to drive with their kids because they want their entire family to die. Troubled, troubled, troubled.

13

THE BOOZE WILL never go away, Mom. I turn on the TV, watch Friday Night Lights, and see Tim Riggins chugging beer after beer, flask after flask. Then I go to the store to get my fix.

There is something so magical about alcohol–maybe it's the way the sugar molecules are put together, in such a tangy and sour fashion. Maybe it's the cold feel of the beer on the lips, running down all organs, ending at the liver. Maybe it's the iciness of the bottle on a hot summer day. Or the way the liquid foams to the top, then settles back down. It's heaven on Earth, Mama. A heaven curated by ethanol and ethanol only.

If you really want to know the truth, I don't really like being trans. I'm not cut out to be a trans guy–I'm just cut out to be a regular, old fashioned dude. No one can tell I'm trans, Mom. Not a soul on this Earth. They all think I'm trying to be a good actor, pretending and all sorts of stuff. But the truth is I don't try hard–or try at all–to pretend to be a man. It comes naturally to me, Mom, just as wind comes naturally in the aftermath of a tornado, as Redwoods come naturally to the forest, as salt comes naturally to the Pacific Ocean. This is how natural it is for me to be a guy in this world.

Childhood ended at puberty, when my body was streaming against its bones and caves of skin, pleading to be a man. But childhood also ended when I picked up the bottle–at age 12–and drank my first sip of alcohol–a shot of Stolichnaya, some of the best, most pungent Russian vodka on the market. I'll never forget the first taste of real alcohol outside of church wine: the vodka burned my throat and seemed to burn all of the internal organs. But in a good way, a way that made the warm and full of life. And then a few shots later–at the age of 12–all of my social walls went down, and I could make out with anyone of my liking, kiss any boy ready for the taking, and make the best, liveliest conversation possible. That feeling of warmth didn't stop, Mom. It still runs wild to this day–and runs wild in other people–other people who love booze just as much as I do.

Booze is my first church. I worship alcohol like none other.

PEOPLE ARE VULTURES. WE are absolute monsters. We eat away at each other, hoping our corpses will rot in the dirt. People are vicious. We lionize those who secretly commit evil but ostracize those who don't fit in and have good hearts beating under their skin. The world is a crapshoot–it's a game of luck, a poker round at Monte Carlo. Success is determined by who your parents are, and not your actual gift. Well, maybe some of your gift. Talent etched in lines of literature.

My head is swarming with trauma–trauma from college years, which weren't so precious after all. College was a glorious maelstrom of change. There were good things about it, and bad things too.

Trauma is horrible–it is not a gift, but rather one 500 calorie serving of hell. Trauma inhabits the brain as a hurricane would take over a city without any prior notice and dwarf it in waves and winds. Trauma hides in the deep recesses of the mind until it unleashes itself over and over again, repetitively, when there is nothing to see–nothing to hear–except for the voices of old perpetrators, past friends, past events that stabbed at the heart with a dagger made of the finest, rawest metal.

Flashbacks start to stream through the mind as a river would in the deepest valley, a river bending, with undulating currents that never seem to stop–never fail–never disappear into the ground or vaporize into air. Flashbacks of things that hurt, that make the heart heavy, that renders one unable to love, unable to laugh, unable to smile at the small things, the finer things, the things that engulf the present moment.

These flashbacks are repetitive, they are silent–no one can see them–and they are fearful. When trauma is in full force, the memories of other things past start to dissipate too, and false memories can arise as well. A tortured memory is not a good look for a young person, let alone a young man wishing to write novel after novel after novel, letting the world in on secret plots and rife characters.

Trauma is an enemy, but it is also a friend, because *repressed* trauma–memories that only come back after years of not-knowing–serve as a lighthouse guiding one to the truth of their history. When memories are, indeed, suppressed, the beholder is unaware of their past life, unaware of things that are rotting their brain, unaware of the real source of anger and shame.

Trauma can make someone bedridden for days on end–only waking up to drink coffee, read five minutes of news, shower, then crash into bed again, suffering the visuals of flashback after flashback. These flashbacks are so intense that they eat up my every day, putting me silent, sitting on a couch and staring at the wall–staring at my inner demons but really, just staring at nothing, Mom.

Trauma has been swallowing my body whole. I can spend dozens of minutes–even hours–staring into space, replaying these memories that froze my mind and are now torturing it. I've never understood the true meaning of trauma until now.

HUMANS ARE INHERENTLY CRUEL. People are inherently scared of what is different, and shudder at the thought of someone who stands out. People like to *other* those who they feel don't belong. What is perceived as different suddenly becomes something that is wrong, and something to be ashamed of. Weirdness is a harsh barometer–those who are freaks have less friends, and those who have friends spend all of their time bullying others into thinking they are freaks.

My friend went to a bar in Tampa tonight with a date–a lesbian. The lesbian started talking smack about my friend behind her back, to the point where the bouncer took my friend out of the club and told her that it was best to go home, because this cruel person–who happened to be a therapist–couldn't stand the thought of spending time with someone who went against the grain.

People call *me* weird, but I don't care. How can someone like me possibly be normal? Partly raised in the Middle East, with a stint of learning-how-to-drink in Russia, I became a female track star only to find out that I wanted to change genders. As a man, I loathe most sports–except for soccer–and just stick to weight lifting. Athletics is screwed. Poetry is where it's at. Literature is where the world belongs–where people become rich in knowledge and warmth. The world of the Literati is a universe of books and letters that transcends everything known to man. What is written down will be recorded for eternity, and what is recorded for eternity is etched into the literary cannon with hints of Hemingway and Camus.

People make stories, and stories change people. Stories work for the greater good–but not the one about my friend in Tampa. That one can be tossed into the proverbial garbage can, alongside the lesbian who made her feel like a piece of shit.

There is too much cruelty in the world, Mom. Innocent children are being bombed in Gaza and they shudder at the thought of both *not* eating breakfast the next day and knowing that the Palestinian version of Cheetos might be blown to bits alongside their parents. My friend gets made fun of, *I've* been made fun of, weirdos are made fun of and Saudi bombs keep ripping over Yemen. Men rape and pillage at will then get let onto the Supreme Court. Women in Afghanistan are hit, continuously, by the Taliban. Trans women are dying too early in life–and they are dying by knife wounds and gunshots (not the self inflicted kind). A trans man was murdered a few months ago in North Carolina by a man who he thought was a date.

Bipolar patients are dying earlier in life–one decade earlier–and trans people are dying earlier too. Our life expectancies are shortened from stress. Cancer patients in Gaza can't get access to chemotherapy. They *haven't* had access to chemotherapy in years, even before this godforsaken conflict. Sweet people are suicidal and those verging on evil are making *others* feel suicidal. Gay teenagers want to take their lives. *Trans* teenagers want to take their lives.

Humans are so cruel that we subject each other to genocide, warfare, poverty, and discrimination. We tease one another. Taunt each other. Mock all others over our godforsaken breaths. Humans are nasty. We're cruel, Mom–as cruel as a Russian winter, in the dead of December, when street sweepers are manically brushing snow aside and sipping on borsch. Cruel, cruel, cruel. When your eyelashes freeze together because you forgot to wipe them from the shower. Cruel, cruel, cruel.

14

I am helping my landlord's nephew start a DJ company. His name is Giulio. He lives up above me, in DC, next to the pines and oaks of Cleveland Park. Next to the National Cathedral. Next to the Washington Ballet, and next to the Naval Observatory. Next to a dozen embassies, next to cafes where Post journalists meet up with diplomats. Where track runners race the mile at Sidwell Friends.

Giulio is ethereal: his hair is short and curled, and he is from Florence. Giulio is, indeed, mostly Italian. His English is punctured with staccato and the occasional *bravo*: times when he'll applaud something you say, whether it's about how to capture a girl, or take a photo in the fall. He only drinks mineral water, bought from Wegman's. Usually at 11:30 p.m., just before the stroke of midnight, I drive him to the store so he can pick up his week's supply. We lounge on rooftops together and hit up Georgetown.

Giulio is young, and still has a lot of learning to do. But he has a good heart, and doesn't wish unwell on anyone. He is 23. He works at a cafe nearby, and a restaurant at night, as a host and barista.

Giulio doesn't know that I have bipolar. He doesn't know that I take more than three pills each day just to try to cure some disease in my head. He doesn't know that I was in rehab.

I don't want him to know these things. I don't want him to think that these horrific things even exist–that hallucinations and psychosis can be real. I don't want him to ever go through what I went through. I don't want him to suffer, and I don't want him to be in pain.

At night I ask him about his playlists. Whether he's mixing things right, whether he's playing techno or Buddha bar. I ask him about jazz, and classical songs, and hip hop. I tell him to make business cards with a logo on it–a logo I can source from the web. I tell him to make a one page brochure, advertising his services. I tell him to go to venues, cold footed, and give them his name. I tell him that much of business is done by word of mouth–that the customers he sees at Tatte and the Oyster Bar will eventually be his clients.

I don't think Giulio knows what it's like to have your brain be disconnected from reality–to escape the present universe for a one that is darker and much colder in nature. This is, in a way, a textbook definition of psychotic. He will–with all of my hope–never know the meaning of that word, and I like to keep it that way.

In the back of my mind, when we walk to the National Cathedral at midnight with a beer in hand, I wonder if he'll ever know the hell I've been to. I wonder if he knows what Hurt Capital is. I wonder if he will ever witness any pain–the kind of pain that wrenches your heart, that distorts your thinking. That throws a curve ball into your feelings.

I pray it won't be the case. I pray he'll be this DJ guru, mix music, and find peace at that. I pray he'll earn a decent paycheck in DC. I pray he'll stay lost in the world he has composed for himself: a world where bass is an alpha male and distant piano is a hero.

Someday, I might tell him what hell really looks like, but not now. I will tell him how hell feels: how it smells, how it sounds.

How hell is a dungeon curated by psychotic nightmares and traumatic flashbacks. But not now, Mom. Not now.

It is flurrying in D.C. today. A white blanket unfolds across Georgetown and Glover Park. The National Cathedral is coated in a fine layer of snow and its arches stand out with gargoyles and Catholic sayings. Girls trickle out of the ballet studio and bankers leave early to go back to million dollar townhouses.

D.C. is the best city in the United States, save for New York. In some ways, actually, it outshines New York, as it's trickling with more spies and ex KGB henchmen. The foreigners in D.C. know what's up–they know how to eat Ethiopian food right, they know how to say hello in Chinese and bye in Italian, all the while making conversation in French.

The city is alive below this white blanket–it's not as bustling as Manhattan, but it's rather a sleepy enclave of diplomats. If you know the right people in DC–which you definitely do, Mama–then your life is turned upside down by sessions in emergency crisis rooms and negotiations with the Taliban. *You* can negotiate with anyone, Mom.

Can you negotiate with my bipolar? Can you sit across from Big Bipolar at a wooden table and ask it for better neurotransmitters, calmness, better meds. Can you plead with it to not wrack my mind into an eventual state of cognitive decline.

Did you know that almost everyone–in fact *everyone*–with bipolar enters cognitive decline at the end of their life? What makes the process happen faster is repeated bouts of mania and hypomania–these will fry the mind to death. Psychosis will also do a number on it to the point where it becomes unbearable to live in our brain. All of these things make us more susceptible to memory issues at the end–and also to interactions with other meds. As a population, we generally are more stressed out than others over the course of our lifetime, which subtracts from our life expectancy.

In fact, the life expectancy of someone with bipolar is around 67 years old. *Sixty-seven,* Mama. The average life expectancy of someone in the US is around 77 years these days, so bipolar patients can expect to live a decade less than others.

This is sad but refreshing. I don't want to be plagued by the world's worst ills towards the end of life–I just want to see all of my existence disappear in one shot. I don't want cognitive decline. I don't want to sit here in D.C. all the time mulling over death.

I miss the days when I was scrambling for my life in an empty Tel Aviv meat market, past midnight. Those were the days to be alive. Those are the times I crave. I'm not meant to be unstable, laying low in the nation's capital. In Hurt Capital, playing Xbox and writing tortured poetry. That's not me, Mama. The real Isaac is the one in Tel Aviv–the one hunting for a next story to tell at a teatime somewhere on the coast. The real me is in Cyprus, clubbing in New York, fiending for better horizons somewhere across the Atlantic. Not sullen in Washington.

The mind works in mysterious ways, Mom. The mind will surprise you. Jab you in the rib. Think of things that did happen when they really *didn't.* Think of things that never happened when they really *did.*

15

THE PILL BOTTLES are now rappers. *Eminem. Jay Z. Kanye. Drake. Jack Harlow. Mac Miller.*

But this time, they didn't have my back. They didn't make me happy. They didn't prevent my hypomania. They didn't save me from catatonic depression. And I didn't have their back either. I took the bottles and threw them onto the bathroom floor until every little capsule spilled across the tiles.

Suddenly, the floor was littered with different colors: mostly white, but some orange and red in between. I took my feet and crushed each pill until it was made of pill dust: white embers and ashes to be thrown into the wind. Eminem had disappeared. Jack Harlow was dead. Jay Z had fought me and lost, and I couldn't fucking believe it. I then went to the kitchen, opened the fridge and undid the lid to the high pulp orange juice. I took the juice and splashed it across my one bedroom floor, until every carpet and wooden panel had gotten a taste of citrus. No longer would I have to drink high pulp stuff; no longer would my stomach have to deal with its heavy texture. I could now drink lemonade at night, or raspberry iced tea, or fat free milk—not the whole kind. I was finally free, Mom. I was free after all these years.

I think I have lots of fake friends. This is something I noticed just recently. I went to a writing retreat for two weeks and very few people asked me to hang out. Very few asked about my whereabouts. In fact, the only person that initiated a text was Keya, because something was happening with our cat.

The world is made of phonies. There are phony people everywhere. At the grocery store, in bars, near restaurants, in hospitals, around the neighborhood. Phony people are scared of bipolar. They don't know what it's like to be manic–to be psychotic–to be disconnected from reality. Phony people laugh at people like me. They make fun of us–tease us, taunt us at every turn, because deep down, they are scared, and they are cowards. They are fucking cowards, Mom.

Phony people should visit a psych ward. They should visit a rehab, and take care of patients there. They should study the kinds of pills available on the market. Phony people should read up on lithium doses. They should feel the brunt of a needle and understand how to inject testosterone. Phony people need a redo. A glow up.

Phony people are tacky. But I'm not tacky, Mom. Not one bit.

I can count on my hand the amount of people who are real to me. You are one of them, despite your talks about me having to get a job and be serious all the time. Helen is another, and that's because we were in the same womb together, and literally–quite literally–when I am very unwell, I hear her voice play over and over in my head, telling me that I am unwell, until I can't block it out. Giulio is like my little brother, so he's not really a friend, he's more like family.

There have been other people who have flung themselves into my life and then carelessly gone with the wind. Thieves. Bigots. Nerds. I *have* had my fair share of women, and men, at that. Love life has never really been an issue. But right now I don't have a love life, and I'm dreaming of all of these heiresses who I want in my bedroom, and it's preventing me from going out into the real world and finding someone.

I'm not well enough to do that yet. But I'm better, Mama.

I don't like to call people fake, per se, because I want to give them the benefit of the doubt. There are tons of people out there who don't act maliciously–who do, in fact, have very decent hearts, just like Giulio. I just can't seem to keep that many relationships down, or at least I *used* to have that problem.

To slander *everyone* as fake would mean that there is some greater issue with me, and that I think the world is a conspiracy. That's not the case, even despite the mania and psychosis. I don't think the world is some super twisted realm, although I *do* sometimes live in Hurt Capital, which is why this book came into existence.

Despite living in Hurt Capital, I do my best to smile. The days go by in my late twenties and I see people change for the good: I see Helen get a job and slowly rise to what will be the top of a corporate ladder. I see our younger sister bake really good sourdough and cherish her career as well. I see you and Dad soften–just a bit–and stand for us not as guardians or whip-crackers pushing us to Ivies, but as quasi-senior citizens hoping to get one last movie in with us. I see my landlord's nephew rely on me to start his DJ company. Despite the perils of my own mind, I manage his business like a pro.

But most of all, I see friends stay in my life. They trickle in slowly–right after college–and stick around. There's fewer good-byes and more hellos. More constant hellos, over months and even years–which boggles me, because moving around so much as a kid I could never hold a friend down for more than one Foreign Service rotation at a time. My best friend in the entire world–the person who understands me the most–is a very straight man who was born as a boy into this world. He presides over my kingdom, despite moving–despite being away–he counsels me in thought. We discuss women, and Israel-Gaza, and Russia, and henchmen. I think he understands the intricate layout of Hurt Capital. I think he understands the foreign streets I walk–the alleyways I dodge and cobblestone I tread. I think he understands that my reality was borne grimmer than most. Someday–someday–I'll thank him for that.

While some friends stay, others leave. I wouldn't call them friends, but rather beautiful, smart women–just like you–who were somewhat romantically involved with me. These women, as I wanted, can recite Kant off the top of their head. They took Classics classes at Yale and know the difference between Cartesian theory and moral absolutism. They wear Tiffany's, just like you. They prance around in coastal cities and share dalliances, in perfect sepia tone, on Instagram. They capture roses in Central Park and dance to Aviici at festivals. They are perfect–just like you–and remind me of who a wife should be.

One day I'm going to find a version of this woman and stick to her like tar on a piece of the finest mahogany slab. I'm going to wed her, and we're going to read Shakespeare together, and then we're going to laugh at Infinite Jest–because that book was a piece of shit, if you ask me. But Foster Wallace is my competition, and his words were perhaps bigger than the ones I'm using here. He was a literary genius, and he was troubled–and–well, well I'm trou–I'm troubled, but I promise you Mama, I'm a literary genius as well. Just remember that. Remember that, please. If there's one thing in this world I can give you, it's my literary intellect. Not my cognitive functioning–not any of my executive skills–not my emotional IQ–not my social adeptness. I can be miserable at some of those things. But I will deliver words to you on a silver plate–a plate adorned by the best adjectives and nouns and verbs in the business. Parts of this manuscript will make your jaw drop and heart stop. I'm in it for you, Mama, not for anyone else.

My neighbors just threw a dinner party and didn't invite me. I don't really like them–I don't like people my own age–so I tend to take my car and joy ride to Dulles airport just for fun, just to avoid them. And in the car, I think about this book, and the repercussions of it being published. I think of all of the conservatives who will want to ban it, and I think of all of the Instagram DMs I will get telling me to repent to God. I already get a few of those, you know, from my writing for the Washington Blade. I think of the people who will say that my gender is a delusion, not knowing that being a man is the one thing that makes me stable. One of my neighbors said that I was the creepy guy who lived in the basement–and, if you really want to know the truth, that set me off a bit, because I think I just appeared mysterious to her, and scared her. And come to think of it, I think I scare people a lot–I think I have that effect on them, but I'm not sure why. Some do say I am mysterious–and while I don't actively try to be mysterious, I also don't feel like pouring my heart and thoughts out to every stranger I meet on the street. To be honest, I think that most people I meet aren't as brilliant as I am, and simply just don't understand the way I think and perceive the world. I don't think they understand literary excellence, and I don't think they could tell a hyperbole from the truth. So I stay away, and do my own thing, and try to find other brilliant minds, bu it's ha–it's hard–when you're as brilliant as I am. Sometimes I think I'm too brilliant for my own good–that I'm so inordinately smart that I really don't belong on all of these streets with these peasants–that I instead belong in a universe crafted for Camus and Einstein. But that universe doesn't exist, and never will, so instead I find myself in Hurt Capital, where shitheads who don't know the meaning of *realism* call me creepy. Just leave me alone, please. Leave me the fuck alone, unless you've read *Song of Solomon* ten times over, or unless you've won a Pulitzer or Booker Prize. Then I'll talk to you.

You know, Mom, I'm an old soul at best–stranded between books of Kant and teatime talk of World War II. I really don't belong with people my own age–not even at 29, or 30, or 35. I prefer to make conversation with Vietnam War vets and talk to women who have been through it all–been through the Great Depression, breast cancer, divorce, and the overdoses of beloved children. I prefer to read Toni Morrison when I can, and make money along the side–taking classes on private equity and constitutional law and poetry. I prefer to write verses to attract women, and not do anything else to win them over. I do like Drake though, and listening to his songs, which is the one thing that keeps me young. There is nothing like *Take Care* on a rainy day, or *Marvin's Room* at midnight.

Most people at my age, at 29, haven't been through what I've been through–they haven't been psychotic, they haven't been manic, they haven't been married and then divorced, they haven't seen another person die, they haven't been to rehab, they haven't been hit by a car in Cyprus, they haven't traveled to 35 countries, and they haven't changed genders, let alone changed it in the Middle East. They haven't written as well as I write, and they aren't as brilliant as I am. They also don't have an identical twin–a twin you thought you would mirror your whole life, only to find out that she was the opposite of what lays deep in my heart and mind. Most people, therefore, inherently don't understand me and my life, and will never be able to understand it. So I stay away from people who are too young, too naive, too foolish for their own good. I surround myself, sometimes, with thugs, and drug dealers, and raging alcoholics, mainly because they get what I have been through.

The question of fake friends will never really be solved in my head: I can't differentiate who is real to me and who isn't. Who is true and who is not. Who is there during fair weather: when I'm in a National Geographic documentary, when I'm writing good columns for the Yale Daily News, and when I'm offering sexual favors.

Honestly, I think that most people don't give a damn about my life, and mostly just care about theirs. But I can't help but think that there might be something wrong with me–something that turns me off to other people. Perhaps I make people feel strange, or perhaps I'm merely too threatening for others–maybe for a trans man, I have too much money, too much clout in Virginia politics, too many good looks. Maybe I just say the wrong things. It's a tragedy, because I wouldn't hurt a fly. Unless some monstrous fly was attacking me, like those monstrous men at Nanny O'Briens, or like that rich Democrat who kept on touching me too much, or like all of the conservatives who think that sodomy is a fucking crime.

I'm tired of all of these phonies--phonies raised to tell me lies but speak harsh truths behind my back. Harsh truths about how they feel towards a trans man. A trans man who has richer parents than they do. A trans man who is smarter than them. More brilliant. More creative. Who has a supportive twin that they want to date all the damn time. Stop asking me to date Helen. Go get her number yourself if you really want to court her. Fake. Fake fucks. Phonies. They're fair-weather friends. Friends around for the good weather—the money and champagne and strip clubs and promotions and the sex and trips to Amsterdam—but not around for the bad weather—the bipolar and the nervous breakdowns and the divorce and the ugliness of being trans. Friends who like your literary accomplishments but are envious of them behind closed doors. Friends who manipulate and say subtle things to get under your skin. They know how to bite silently, Mom.

I'm sick of them. Sick of each and every last one of them. They can fuck off into the horizon and gallop past by castle of love and warmth. I've built a kingdom of loyalty but very few people want to join it. My true friends—a rarity—won't be afraid to tell me what's up. To slap me around, demean me, say I'm fucking up in some way. Point out exactly how life is unraveling in the current moment. Sometimes, the people who make you feel the worse (with the most savage advice) are the ones who need to stick around. Not the ones complimenting your every move, hanging on so they can be Helen's next nonexistent boyfriend.

Fake fucks. I miss Keya. Keya wasn't fake to me at *all*, Mom. She was real. As real as can be. Keya wasn't a phony. She loved me even when I was being a jackass and when I was a manic madman. She loved me through thick and *thin*, Mama. And there's no turning back. At all.

I think I've borne too many scars from living in this world, Mom. There are two literal ones—on my chest, cut neatly into semi bending lines. But there are other scars that can exist. Hidden ones, that tear at the mind. Hidden scars are the worst kind of scar to get—usually spurred by trauma, no one else can spot these quiet scars. If a man stabs my eye—like Salman Rushdie's eye was stabbed—then at least people know Salman has been hurt, know he's been swathed by an Iranian fanatic. Know he was in pain because of the blowback from the words in his novels. There's a story to tell.

Human cruelty is limitless, but Keya was by far the least cruel person I've ever met. She didn't have a drop of harm in her blood–no mean bone in her body. In fact, the perfect couple is made of a man who has been wounded hundreds of times and of a woman who has never wounded anyone–and can cure any scar tissue with the proper amount of hugs and bedtime conversations.

But Keya is gone now, thrown into the random gusts of the wind–untethered–away. She's *away.* That's it. She is betrodden to other people–other names–other families out there, waiting to reel her in. She's not mine, anymore. She's fodder for someone else now. And that's the most painful thing of it all.

MY IDEA OF A good time is curling a woman up in my arms and reading Faulkner–together–from the same book–while Miles Davis is playing and after I've made her carbonara. There is something so comforting–so utterly soothing–about a Southern novel. Sure, the South experienced too much turmoil. And too much cruelty. The South, indeed, was a touchstone for cruelty–a gate into slavery–into America's worst sin. But despite this looming mistake, the South is a source of comfort for America.

The Northeast? The Northeast is for fast talkers, fast walkers, and Manhattanites just waiting to bitch at the next passerby. The West is for mountaineers, adventurers, climbers, and Seattelites with too much coffee. The Midwest is a sorry land–but a land that holds our Puerto Rican grandmother. The Midwest is made of corn and Chicago.

But the South, Mom, the South I like for its comfort. Not for its bigotry, for its backwardness, or for its Civil War legacy. I like the collard greens, the slow and soothing accent, and grits–the grits are the best.

And Faulkner sure as hell knew how to take one town–one town in Mississippi–and blow it up into one hell of a story. On my imaginary date, I'm reading *As I Lay Dying* next to this stated fireplace, and we are in each other's arms, and we are taking Faulkner in slowly, word by word, reading his lines to each other–and we are rotating lines, and turning the pages together, and cuddling next to the warmth of the fire.

Faulkner is speaking to us, and we are speaking to Faulkner, and for one second–for one hot second–I can pretend like I actually belong in the South, like the South likes me, a fast talking, fast walking, mission headed trans man. The truth is, the South doesn't like me Mom, but I like parts of it–and it doesn't like any of me.

But I sure as hell retain my right to like Faulkner, and to like the lady in my embrace, and to like the fireplace.

Literature makes the world go round. How many times will that be said? Faulkner makes the world go round, *As I Lay Dying* makes the world go round, Kafka makes the world go round, and Yeats does, as well. Speaking of Southern comfort, there is nothing more comforting than the look of words on paper, and the weight of pages in a book. Books are what cure evil, and books will save us all.

Trauma is harder to talk about. Trauma comes back through stories—stories that play through the mind, flashbacks of *this* and *that*. Remnants of bad times. Memories that cling to your cortex like sap on the roughest bark in Vermont.

THERE IS A WOMAN in my past life who raises people well. She cultivates them, and gives them every benefit of the doubt. She has a way with the English language, and appreciates others who do as well. One day, I'll thank her for everything she helped me with.

I once fell in love with an older woman. She was in her late thirties, and had straight hair. Her body was quite fine, but her personality rocked the boat. There was one thing connecting us:

our love for literature. She loved literature like none other, Mom, and she had a way with words–just like you. And this woman was made of absolute steel–she could have built a skyscraper herself if she wanted to. In downtown Manhattan. But instead she chose to teach writing, and to teach literature, and to teach good books. And for that, I am forever grateful.

We both loved Hemingway. And Camus. And other authors. And we both wrote poetry in our free time, and submitted to journals. And we both wanted to get MFAs. But we never did.

16

Most Americans live in mediocrity. They don't realize they are mediocre because everyone around them is as well. They're not blessed with any kind of greatness–any incredible stroke of luck or talent. These Americans just idle by, occasionally messing up in some way, like yelling a racial slur at a bar, and occasionally making good decisions, like birthing a child who they won't hit or manipulate. Some Americans fall shorter than others. Some do, indeed, curse their kids, and lie at a job, and mock others. Vote for Trump and call it a day.

Most average Americans go about their daily lives doing the same exact thing: putting coffee in the pot, making a sandwich for their kid, clocking in at a 9 to 5 in somewhere as boring as Scranton or Durham. Occasionally, these American adults will go out at night with friends, and crack open a beer and–who knows–maybe become swingers for the night, trading spouses. That's the most exciting it gets for them.

No one should ever be tacky. The world should not be run by tacky people. It should be run by *un*tacky people: people who live their truths and don't give a shit what society says. And it should be run by smart people: people who have read Kant and passed calculus and know about emotional intelligence.

Most Americans don't know what it's like to be hypomanic in the Jordanian desert. They don't know what it's like to change your body somewhere near Aqaba–somewhere in Jerusalem–somewhere in Tel Aviv. They don't know what it's like to have racing thoughts amid sand dunes and desert wadis, where the touch of hookah and a cold Coke can grace your lips at any ill forgotten time.

The lust for life is just too real right now. Even though I feel like I'm in the pits–in the pits trying to ward off racing thoughts and *more* mania and rapid speech and psychosis–and trying to ward off transphobes and transphobic slurs and *homophobic* slurs–I still love people too much. Love life too much. I love a pot of morning coffee, served just at seven a.m., when the sun's rays are finally making travel across the Earth. I love the smile on a lover's face when she lays under me. I love the chuckle of the waiter at the beer bar next door. I love the way a pen feels across the finest parchment paper. I love the kick of a soccer ball from the corner. I love a far aunt's face when she says she's healthy again. I love the smirk that Nancy Pelosi gives when she knows she has done Trump in. I love the ice rink at Rockefeller Center in the New Year. I love the Empire State. I love New Delhi. I love rickshaw drivers in Mumbai and Goa. I love the men I play chess with. I love everything too damn much. I love the struggle of being trans and bipolar–I love sacrifices in life. I love hurting. I love feeling pain from others because they left or chose someone else over me. I love relationships. I love feeling connected with someone. I love knowing that someone has been through hell and back and still decides to stay here, just like me–just like I do.

I felt inferior again, today, for no apparent reason whatsoever except for the fact that I am trans. Perhaps I will perpetually feel this way, strung in a state of high anxiety and near boredom at myself, wondering why I couldn't be some NFL tight end or famous actor or just regular, not gender-bending high school graduate. Maybe a high school graduate who felt like the body they were born in, and weren't ashamed of it. Maybe someone who *was* indeed tacky, and conformed at every turn–married their high school sweetheart, had kids, worked a regular job in regular suburban America, never had to take any meds until the age of 75.

THE WORLD IS MADE of cruelty. In fact, the world is more cruel than it is good. Some men kill trans women because they are too scared of their attraction to them. Other men beat trans women because they're scared of the femininity that can lie in someone born with male parts.

In South Carolina, recently, a trans man died because a man he was supposed to date killed him. This trans man's name was Jacob Williamson. I wrote a statement on it for the LGBT Democrats of Virginia because I'm a member of the boa–I'm a member of the board, Mama.

People don't like others who are different. They put us on the sidelines, sequestering us to the fringes of society–and *sequester* was a word from the hidden dictionary, and let me see what it means he–let me see what it means here–and Webster says it means to isolate or hide away, so my bipolar mind is good for something after all, Mom–it is good for something. And this hidden dictionary right here is going to skyrocket me to award stages–and I'm gonna win a Pulitzer for you, Mama–just for you–I'm gonna win one someday, so that you know that the son you gave birth to might be sick but is smart, is a liter–is a literary genius, Mom. You will sure as hell know that one day, and I'm going to win a Booker prize as well, and a PEN Faulkner prize too. Then I'm going to write some poetry just for you–just for you–and *that* poetry is going to win a National Book Award.

I'M STILL IN HURT Capital.

The world has gone to shit. Nothing matters. Nothing that is important, that is. The world is not a good place. People are simply too cruel. Too cruel to each other. Too cruel to *me.* I've been teased, taunted, mocked at every turn, Mom. Mocked far too much.

I won't blow my brains out, but Hurt Capital is all too real. Too many men want to hurt other trans men. When cis, straight men see that we are landing more ladies than them–when we are richer than them–when we dress better–when we talk better–when we write better–when we drive a better car, these men get jealous. They get jealous of the fact that a woman can now become one of them and have better things in life. In these cruel mens' eyes, women who try to be men shouldn't have it better off than they do. We shouldn't be wearing better flannel shirts or boots. We shouldn't have a better job, in IT contracting or defense. We shouldn't be writing better verses. And we shouldn't be sleeping with more beautiful women.

Once trans men realize that cis men get jealous, we start to feel like we don't deserve these things too. We start to internalize their jealousy and hate. But the best thing you can do is fight back, Mama. Fight back against what society says about us. This is the epitome of my day: fighting back the words that people are unjustly stuffing down my throat. Fighting back against the ideas and preconceptions that people are also unjustly stuffing through my body.

Cis men can be cruel to me–they can get jealous of the women I'm able to date, they can get jealous of my accomplishments and smarts. This happens all too often. As a trans man in this world, who looks good and writes well, I face stiff competition from other men, and they see me as a threat. This inevitably means that cruelty will arrive at my doorstep–in the manner of a bully on Facebook, or a friend turned enemy, or another kind of foe. Indeed, there are too many enemies–too many foes in this world to count. Some don't see me as competition, but others do. It's hard to make guy friends as a trans man. Many men don't want to admit to the fact that a trans man may be better than them–at sports, at literature, at dating and sleeping with women.

The worst cruelty inflicted on trans men is cis men cockblocking us from beautiful girls.

There is a man named Dan Sutherland who is chasing Keya, and telling her not to hang out with me. I know we're exes, but no one can ever prevent my beautiful Keya from being in my arms, or at least, in the throes and circles of my embrace. Dan Sutherland plays it nice to my face, then shit talks me behind my back. This is what the state of the world has come to: nice guys being mean to other nice guys who are just trying to get by in life.

Dan Sutherland is a pussy ass motherfucking faggot who can suck my future dick, if I ever have one. The Dan Sutherlands of the world ruin the worlds of trans guys like me.

Cis guys don't want trans men to land the best women, Mom. Society has convinced them that *they* are entitled to the Keya's of the world, and not us. *They* deserve the beautiful faces. *They* deserve the wide hips. *They* deserve all of the dates. Just because they were born in the same gender they were assigned at birth. Meanwhile, *we* are supposed to suffer our way through the day, clawing and knocking on bartop counters just to get laid. It's an eternal struggle, but not when I present my literature to the ladies.

They eat me up when I show them the writing I can produce, Mom.

And to tell you the truth, Mom, I think a lot of trans guys are jealous of me. They're jealous of how well I pass. Barely anyone can clock me as trans, Mom. Not a soul knows unless I say something. I got a nice jawline from you and Dad–and I got lots of muscle–and I got a deep, deep voice from the testosterone. All of these other trans guys might be jealous of my money. My family. The family *you* created. It's rare that I'm friends with one.

My transition was something that happened to me eight years ago. I changed my body, changed my voice, and changed my style. That was it. Now I barely think about it–being trans is just a fact of life, but definitely not my entire identity.

Many people are scared of me. They're scared of how well I pass. Of how intelligent I am. Of how much power I hold. Most trans people aren't supposed to hold power, Mom. At least that's what society thinks. And I'm brill–I'm brill–I'm brilliant beyond belief. Just trust me on that, Mama. Trust me.

There are too many enemies to count, Mom. Too many enemies that I didn't even try to hate–just people who are on my bad side, who don't want the best for me. And because of that, I don't want the best for them. Being a trans man, even in America, is hard. It is grueling, it is an open door to all sorts of cruelties by other humans. It is too much to bear sometimes–so much, in fact, that I drown these woes with bottles of beer–countless bottles of beer–too many to count.

I WENT TO BED at 5:20 am this morning after drinking my liver away at a nearby bar. The bar goers and I are festive friends now, or at least festive acquaintances. When they're not making lewd sexual jokes, they are guiding me towards better music: Willie Nelson and Audioslave's "Like a Stone". We listen to Prince on repeat, too. I tell them Prince is sexy no matter what, to whichever gender. His sexiness transcends everything.

Today, I woke up at 5:42pm. I can't help but think that all of the Ivy League graduates I went to school with don't follow this abnormal schedule—they are clerking at law offices and working in private equity. They're at Goldman, or working on a campaign in DC. I wonder if other Yale graduates have ever seen spiders before, materialize out of thin air. I wonder if other graduates have ever had a psychotic break from reality.

In my mind, only a few of them have. And admitting to having been psychotic is like admitting defeat: admitting that your mind can't properly work as well as others, doesn't have the same cogs in the machine as other minds do. Isn't as clean and neat. Can't decipher reality as well as others.

And I'm—I'm having some lithium poisoning again now, Mama. The inside of my mouth is becoming dry and I'm starting to salivate. I can feel it com—I can feel it coming but I'm not going to tell my doctor. If I tell my doctor that the lithium is poisoning me then he might cut the supply, and I really need it Mama. I really need it to stay sane at this point.

Without the lithium, my thoughts race on repeat. This is what it feels like: imagine a fifty foot long tube at CERN, in Switzerland. CERN is known for smashing particles together in all sorts of tubes and discovering new things about science as they go along. So picture a fifty foot long tube. Then picture taking five molecules and sending them through the tube slowly, bit by bit, so they have time for the view. That is what thinking is like on lithium: I may only have a few thoughts per minute, and I'm able to control how quickly they enter and leave my mind.

Now picture the same fifty foot tube. Instead of five molecules, picture fifty going through this metal cylinder, and picture them going really quickly, close to the speed of light. That's what thinking is like when I'm off lithium. It's a nightmare, Mom. It's like fireworks in my brain that won't go away—won't thud to the ground, dead, on the Fourth of July. Machines making noise over and over again and just won't stop—they won't come to a halt, won't take a water break. It becomes torturous. Unlivable. I can't live with the quickness of them all—the chaotic nature of the thoughts. When I was manic for a year, I was inside that fifty foot tube with fifty molecules going at the speed of light. And it hurt like hell.

The lithium poisoning is still going on, Mom. I'm still salivating, after deliberating on all of these sentences. I got myself a nice empty Gatorade bottle to salivate into. It's collecting the remnants of the poisoning quickly, and this episode will probably last for three hours. The best way to deal with these episodes is to put up with the salivation for about an hour, and then force yourself to fall asleep. The salivation will end, but you'll wake up to a puddle of drool next to your face. And that's about the best I can do right now, Mama. That's about the best I can do.

17

IF YOU REALLY want to know the truth, I've only heard things about three or four times in my life.

The first is when I smoked some weed in high school–back in Virginia–with Chad and Brad and Will, names here superfluous–superfluously made up for confidentiality purposes. Superfluous is another word from the hidden dictionary, and let me check what Webster says about it–Webster says that it means unnecessary. I guess this time, the hidden dictionary was close to the truth, but didn't entirely hit the nail on the head.

So let me tell you what I started to hear: cop sirens. They billowed back and forth, with the *eeeh* and *aaah* of the imaginary car. Cop sirens out of nowhere. So everyone at this high school party started to gather around me as I sat in a bush saying the cops were coming. And I was too high to think that it was embarrassing. And the cops never came, Mom. They never came at all. We just kept drinking and making out and laughing hard–and no siren in the world materialized.

Black Lives Matter is a magnificent movement. And to be honest, the cops are the absolute worst. But they chase me around wherever I go, Mama. They sure do.

The second time I heard cop sirens in my ears was several years later–around seven years later, if you really want to know the truth again. It was seven years later, and I was sleeping in our house in Arlington, all nice and tucked in the Virginia backwoods, and I was just sleeping there, and I was sleeping late at night–and trying to go to bed–and the sirens came on in my mind again. Slowly, at first, and then faint, and then they stayed faint, and I put on some classical music–some Beethoven and Pachelbel–and took some hard stuff to go to sleep before anything bad would happen.

The third time I heard cop sirens was waking up from that godawful dream where I also saw a spider racing at me. As the spider was racing at me, the cop sirens were playing that morning in my head as well, and disappeared within a few seconds. There was no police car around–no Metropolitan Patrol of greater Washington DC. Just that noise–that ambiance–the *eeeh* and the *aaah*, the soft yearning for an officer to pull up and give me a speeding ticket. But no speeding ticket was deserved. None at all, Mom.

The fourth time I heard cop sirens I'm not sure of–there might have been a fourth time in there. I think there was. But I've seen so much and experienced so many things in life that I forget when that fourth time happened, to be precise. I think it did.

Anyway, I don't hear cop sirens *that* much–and barely at all–but when I do, the whole world turns upside down. Suddenly, my brain is damaged and challenged to the max. I'm just yearning for survival. Yearning for survival out here, Mama. It's just you and I–just you and I–never forget that. Promise me you'll never forget that. You and I.

I'm manic right now. Manif off of life,, manic off of energy. Manic off of my neighbor's cat–that silly thing that we adorned with lights and fur. I want to see you in a place of success. I want you to make millions, just as you make awards, to the tune of a drum beat. I want you to lobby for Kazakhstan, and never look back. I want you to make 500,000 off of a deal with the Emiratis.

I want you to buy Gucci dresses in Prague. I want you to wear Gucci *heels* in Florence. I want you to marry, once Dad dies, a private equity executive in New York. Who wears Gucci. I want you to take his helicopter to the Hamptons and lord over 800 guests in fake dresses. I want you to be queen–to be supreme, be the lead. I want you to reign.

I will reign in literature, Mom. I know every m-dash known to man, I know every clause known to humankind. I can make a girl weep or smile over one verb. I can make someone laugh with one noun.

I know how to write, and I will write perfectly, to you–and to no one else.

I am sick of pretending. Pretending that I am normal. That I am sane. I am not sane, and I am not normal, and I am not stable. I am Isaac. I am one with myself. I am Alice Wells's son.

I don't like my life right now. I'm too bogged down down by other people–I'm too bogged down by other occurrences. Chelsea Football games at the bar in Arlington. Frisbee on the National Mall. Taking care of a foster puppy in Cleveland Park. I wish I could write like Toni Morrison–write about a years' all struggle–about slavery at the height of the 20th century–in Ohio, with an insurance man at that. I wish I could write about abortion, and about pregnancy, and about alcohol–not in the rehab sense, but in the way that would make a woman turn her eye towards a man, when he was two Martinis deep and eyeing her throat/face. I wish I could write about it.

The world around me doesn't make sense–I can't distinguish what is real from what is fake. I live in Hurt Capital–I live in a slum where beggars see no mercy and liars see no truth. Where druggies can't get their next fix, where prostitutes have to make do with pleasantries. I don't feel as if I belong here–I don't feel as if I belong on Earth, yet I desperately do not want to leave. I love the people around me too much–I am too transfixed by their smiles, their frowns, the wrinkles on top of their eyebrows. I wonder what makes some around me age more than others–if they have, indeed, grappled with their own form of disease, or if they have seen a loved one change genders, or walk into the unknown. I wonder if some of those around me do not want to leave Earth, and if they have ever tried to put that plan into action. I'd want to help them, or reach out some sort of hand.

I've started volunteering at the crisis text line.

I reached out to one of my freshman year roommates. I reached to another one a few months ago, and heard some utterances that I wish I never wanted to hear in the first place. My bipolar was unmedicated freshman year, and I appeared a maniac–quite literally oscillating moods, from happy to depressed, within minutes, just like a spoke goes from up to down on a wheel. I came off as a lunatic–a chaotic woman, one beset with angst. I'm no longer a woman, but I still am chaotic, and it's easier to be chaotic in this gender versus the other. Chaotic men are viewed as archetypes of their own sex: boys and young adults and middle aged fools who race around in their life like a cheetah chasing raw meat, like a mouse avoiding a trap. Chaotic men are animals–we are mammals fiending for the next prey. We yell at friends out of joy–and sometimes bedlam–and pioneer into the night, pounding tequila and shooting up all sorts of stuff.

I've never shot anything up, but I've definitely thought about it. Anthony Bourdain is a hero of mine, and I got his initials tattooed on my back just like that–just like that–A.B., nice and square. They are etched into my skin now, and his spirit lives in my body. *He* certainly shot some stuff up his arm in his life, he shot a lot of that heroin up, and I'm a bit jealous, I'm a bit jealous that he got that high, I wish *I* got that high, and the closest I got was top surgery, when these docs just gave me a boatload of oxytocin, and I took some here and there–day by day–to get rid of the pain, and then when the pain went away, well there was a pill in my body, and it felt *too* good, *too* special, *too* fun. So I stopped, right then and there, and said goodbye to opioids.

To tell you the truth, Mom, I really don't belong here. I don't belong on Earth, with the bipolar, with my whacky mind, with gender bending, and other things. The world hates me, as is, point blank. They hate trans people like me. The moment I put my arm around a beautiful straight girl, a cis guy gets jealous. Especially if that girl has money, and also went to an Ivy league, and is woke, just like me–just like your son. But something in me still wants to be here. If I wanted to kill myself I would have done so a long time ago–years and years ago. But that's just not how I roll, Mama. You raised a killer.

18

LET ME TELL you, in abundant detail, about the drugs that preoccupy my bathroom cabinet. In order of importance (least to greatest): let's start with propranolol. Propranolol 20mg. This drug will inhibit the physical symptoms that come with anxiety. It'll make sure, for 3 hours–and 3 hours only–that your fingers won't sweat and your heart won't race. Propranolol is ideal for a violin soloist at a top tier concert in Boston. Maybe with the Boston Philharmonic or something. Plagued by performance stress, Propranolol will make sure their fingers can touch strings without any perspiration clinging to them.

Next up is Gabapentin. This is the mildest form of anti-anxiety drug known to man. It's colloquially known in some circles as a joke, mainly because its effects are so mild. I'll take a Gabapentin maybe once in a blue moon to go to sleep. Or to just feel a tad bit more relaxed for two hours or so.

After Gabapentin is Ativan. Ativan is a benzo, short for benzodiazepines. Benzos are some of the most addictive drugs known to man, but they don't really catch up to me that much. If I were a true addict, benzos would be the last on my list of pills–the holiest of them all. But they're not. I only used Ativan, for one month, to go to sleep. That's it, really. That's all there was to it.

The fourth drug on the list is Xanax. Known as a killer, Xanax can have people hooked so much that they go into short or long term psychosis in withdrawal. It can make people have seizures. It can make people stop breathing when they drink two bottles of wine with it. Xanax for me is also just a sleep drug–something I've strangely never been addicted to. I should have been hooked on it a long time ago, but addiction to this classy benzo has evaded me. I only use it to go to sleep, and can go weeks forgetting that I even took it.

Fifth is Lamictal. Lamictal is a mood stabilizer. A classic one. A pill that helps you get from depressed to happy to depressed and back to stable again. Lamictal does wonders for my brain, but it's kind of like a constant–something that's always been there, something that prevents the worst of depressive states from ever happening. And it's done the trick, for many, many years Mom. Many years. Ten to be precise.

The sixth med (and the second most important one) is Risperidone, also known as Risperdal. Risperdal is an anti psychotic that works to the nth degree–it quiets a robust inner monologue in the head and prevents you from having *too* many delusions. Or too much psychosis. Or entering an entire psychotic state. When I'm not on Risperdal, my entire world crashes. I feel like running away. I feel like abandoning friends and family. I feel like giving my whole life up to something else. A greater power. Or heaven. But when I'm on this drug, everything is stable.

The last med is lithium. I know what you're gonna say. You're going to say that there are books dedicated to lithium, that there are things called *lithium diaries*, that the entire world of bipolar revolves around lithium. And it does, Mom. Every last piece of it.

But the lithium makes me feel dull. I can't think, can't concentrate, can't do anything on this damn drug. I'm tired of these fake fucks. FAF. Fake Ass Friends. I just went to a bar and drank my liver away but everyone there seemed to want to get away from me. Perhaps I'm too awkward. Too gauche. Anyways, my mind is trapped on lithium. It makes me miserable, Mama. Miserable as can be.

When lithium stabilizes the brain, it also has a way of damping mood. The lithium itself doesn't make someone entirely, deeply, deeply depressed. But it can make them mildly sad–morose, sullen, and somber. Things that once lit up the mind now fade away–exciting memories come back less and less. The world is, indeed, dull. Dull is the perfect word. Webster defines "dull" as "lacking interest or excitement", and "lacking brightness, vividness, or sheen".

All of the above are true. Life just becomes lacking in everything: sunshine even, bright moods, uplifting songs, cheerful interactions with the other guy barbelling at the gym, smiles exchanged at coffee shops. All of those fade away, and what is left is a world covered in sepia, as if lithium has changed vision from color to black and white.

LIthium, in this sense, goes from being a drug that once saved you, to a drug that prevents you from living your full potential. From being entirely, fully, comprehensively happy. It makes sure that can't happen. So you're left with a tradeoff: take the drug to not go crazy, but take it and expect things to be sad. There lies the crux of the trade off: sad but stable, instead of happy and insane.

A psychiatrist once told me that when I was well, I was miserable, but when I was unwell, I was happy. A similar trade off: wellness with misery over instability with happiness.

These tradeoffs don't make sense to the average observer. They assume that if a bipolar patient is stable, that they will be more happy. But that's just not the case, Mom. Or at least, not the case all of the time. Mania brings elation, confidence, and utter jubilance with the state of the world around us. During mania, we are excited by the smallest of things: bought a new coffee maker? I purchased the finest decaf coffee pods on the market–these coffee pods are better than yours, and drinking this decaf will help me write a Pulitzer prize winning novel, and *you* certainly can't write a Pulitzer prize winning novel, because *you're* a piece of shit and I'm bril–brill–I'm brilliant.

When manic, music becomes lit on fire: songs take on new meanings–new dimensions–new places in our life. Rick Ross becomes an angel, rapping about cocaine and feeding women molly then taking them to bed. Drake becomes the Patron Saint of Rhyme. Even Lil Wayne is a literary genius.

AND NOW I'M–NOW I–NOW I'm feeling a bit hypomanic Mom, and it's 11:00 p.m. in my basement apartment, and I'm starting to feel really excited, and hyper, and I can't contro–I can't control this feeling.

Suddenly, a vision of me being interviewed by Joe Rogan has appeared in my head. We're sitting at his studio in Austin, Texas and I'm dishing the latest details on a book I'm going to write. It's called King of D.C., and it just won a Pulitzer. I won a Pulitzer, Mom. I finally made it. Now Joe and I are laughing because we're making fun of Mitch McConnell. But then I start to stick it to Joe, because he hates trans women, and I love them, and I just *need* to fight him, then fight him some more, and some more. Now he's gripping his black mic, and his headphones are on, and now we're switching subjects to Russell Brand. Russell also has bipolar–did you know that? And I have it too, Mom.

And now I'm feeling more hypoma–I'm feeling more hypomanic, so I'm gong to grab my car keys and drive to Reagan airport and back, so that the mania can slowly ebb. It's 11:10 now.

I should be back before midnight. In the car, I envision myself walking alongside Kanye in LA. We're talking about the Life of Pablo. Then we talk about My Beautiful Dark Twisted Fantasy. I say that the All of the Lights interlude is the best song on the entire album. And All of the Lights is the second best, Power third. Now I'm at a Kanye concert, and I'm seated front row next to Kim. Kris Jenner is next to me as well. We're rapping to Famous and dissing Taylor Swift, but I–I really like Taylor, and I'm the problem–it's me, Mom.

I'm sitting in the car, and I've reached Arrivals at Reagan. I'm jealous–jealous of all the travelers making do with economy seats to go on the trip of their lives. Some will reach Toronto, others will hit LA. LA with Kanye West.

I haven't traveled in years, Mom. I miss the minarets of North Cyprus. The clashing keels of sailboats in Kyrenia. I miss the streets of Paris–walls next to the Seine where you can pontificate with a cheap baguette and brie. I miss the cobblestone alleys of Amsterdam, with weed smoke piling outside cafes in the Red Light District. I miss the stare of women there. I eve miss the brutish winters of Moscow, next to ice rinks laden with hockey prodigies. I miss the touch of vodka on my lips in St. Petersburg. I miss the mountains of Peru–the rolling hills that spell a misty dawn in front of Machu Picchu. But most of all, I miss the calls to prayer in Jerusalem. The ramparts walk over steep walls where you spot kids playing soccer in the ARmenian district. And I miss Rainbow Street in Amman. I miss Turkish coffee at 6pm, brought by a taxi driver enamored with the girl sitting next to me speaking perfect Arabic.

I miss French. I miss the French language. I miss lycee in Islamabad and Delhi. I miss *salut* and *a votre sante.* I miss croissants and Le Marais. I miss a glass of wine on the Champs Elysee.

Mom, I'm in the country again. It's different country this time. I'm on Dad's farm, in the Shenandoah. The wolves here will howl past the break of dawn. I feel at pea–I feel at peace again. So now let me talk about being a twin.

I never felt like Helen's sister, Mom. And I never felt like Phoebe's sister either. I never was a girl. I never was a woman. I never was feminine. I didn't like lip gloss. I didn't like mascara. And I sure as hell didn't like blush. Putting on these things was just a mask to disguise the real man deep inside.

In high school, I had boyfriends. I dated two quarterbacks. I danced at Homecoming. I occasionally kissed the odd girl or two, but mostly stuck to boys. I pretended to be a woman, but it was just one big, giant facade. I was living a lie.

I'm still in the country Mom, and I can hear the beaver in the pond creak on repeat. I can hear a country dog in the distance guarding its owner from doom. I look outside the window at the night sky, and the Big Dipper is shining in a way it can't shine in the city. Orion is at his peak. And I see the black, and these gold bursts–and I see these gold bursts and then I start to feel hypomanic again, so I decide to get in my car and drive through the country. I'm going to take a little country drive to clear my mind. This drive is going to feel so *good*, and I'm going to feel so *sexy*, and I will look up at the pitch black sky and think of all the things I can accomplish.

19

LET ME TELL you a secret: people suffer in silence because they are ashamed of the source of their troubles. And they're embarrassed about the kind of hurt they are experiencing. Other people live in Hurt Capital.

I just visited New Haven. College is a blur of memories–memories both near and far. Some good, others bad. I don't believe the world is a good place, if you really want to know the truth. There is too much cruelty that abounds–too much cruelty in America. Enough to fill up a cup of evil–enough to overcome what is right.

Start with slavery, and work your way from there. African Americans–black people–tortured and put down for no other reason than the color of their skin. Then make your way to the Japanese internment camps, near World War II, where Asian Americans were recklessly and indiscriminately put in mini prisons. Then move on to Hiroshima and Nagasaki, where thousands died and were crippled by atomic bombs. Now look at Stonewall and the state of trans rights in America–our justice is being crippled by Republican lawmakers, GOPers with no hearts, and cruel conservatives.

White people are uncomfortable talking about race. But it's entirely fucked up to think that black people need to shoulder this burden all by themselves–when in reality, *we* are the ones who subjugated them to begin with in this godforsaken country.

It shouldn't be black peoples' burden to pick up the pieces and create a new life for their kin–new generational wealth, new HBCUs, new families, new nonprofits. White people need to do the work of ending racism as well. Yet most faces at Black Lives Matter rallies are, indeed, black–and just that. Few Asians, few latinos, few whites.

I still think, to this day, that slavery has been the greatest moral atrocity America has ever committed. It's our worst sin. Worse than the subjugation of trans lives, gay lives, and all other lives. Slavery lasted, technically, for eighty nine years, but that's only assuming it ended just after the Gettysburg Address. Slavery in other forms kept on existing for centuries to come, and racism predominated the South and Northern regions of the nation, and racism still runs rampant to this very day.

Black men couldn't sit in certain restaurants. Black people had to sit in the back of the bus. Go to different bathrooms. Drink at different water fountains. What kind of fucked up place does *that,* Mama?

I don't think the trans struggle and African American struggle can be compared.. I think our suffering is similar, in many ways, but also different in others. I don't *like* comparing the two. I just like acknowledging that both exist.

I think that both black people and trans people have been *othered.* We have been spat on by greater society–told that we are garbage, rubbish, the latest fetish, too. We are told that we are lesser than. Inferior. Subpar to the average American. Trans people are made to feel like our bodies are repulsive–something that attracts disgust, and not love. Hatred, but not lust. Fear, and not pride. We are shamed. Shamed all the time, Mama. Shamed into thinking we can't love, shouldn't love, may never love at all, or be loved in return. Such shame eats at our core and can drive a man near crazy, if you ask me. It surely has driven *me* crazy at times, Mom.

OTHERS ARE DRIVEN BY jealousy and anger. I don't harbor that much anger anymore–and very little rage. But others, I believe, are envious of our family. The family you and Dad created. Indeed, you guys put together–with hard work and many salaries–a well functioning family unit. We have privileges that others don't, because of you.

I believe that others are sometimes envious of *me*. But it's not my fault that I was born to you and Dad–that you turned out to be an ambassador and Dad turned out to be a CEO of a weapons company. I try to use our privilege in good ways–to stand for the Democratic party, to advance trans rights. This is what is good with the world–the work that we try to do.

It is not my fault that you are my Mom. But I don't see you as an ambassador. I don't see you as a political official. You are the Mom we would take baths with, the woman who read us books as if you were spooning the words from paper into our ears. Harry Potter comes to mind–before J.K. Rowling was cruel herself–before she was a transphobe–you read us Hermione and Harry, and Ron and Snape, to our minds. You loved Harry Potter, and we loved you.

The meaning of life is unclear at this point. The jury is still out. Part of life is not giving a fuck–is living your truth no matter how other people think, feel, or act towards that truth. Another part of life is finding a path–a *way*–a method of moving forward. Each person must find the ethos and lifestyle that suits them well–the hobbies and interests and friends that can bring a smile to their face and purposeful stride to their walk. My purpose is, somewhat, to live as a world citizen–to represent Saudi Arabia and India and Russia in spite of the fact that I am trans and these countries hate changed bodies. My other purpose is to write well, and write a lot, and write beautifully, and eloquently–without fear, without trepidation, without shame. This, I would argue is the easiest thing I do, because when the pen comes down to paper, and when these fingers come down to hit a keyboard, I don't give a fuck what anyone else thinks.

I wouldn't say that my life's purpose is to be trans, though. Other people can represent this identity better–can give better TED talks, better spiels on gender. It's not that I can't do it, I just don't want to most of the time.

My neighbors think I'm a drug dealer. I get confirmation of this from the boy living above me, Giulio, who says they think I sell drugs. After the divorce, I was hanging around some sketchy characters. And one of those characters came onto our property, and the neighbors found out, and now they associate me with him.

I'm not slinging cocaine, Mama. I don't need that to get by.

I FEEL LIKE RUNNING away again. There are dark forces–forces beyond my control–that make me want to pick up a backpack, get in a car, and hit the road again, never to talk to anyone in my life again. Except for you. And Helen. But that's it. I just want to drop everything, get behind a wheel, and start a new life. I want to run away.

Maybe this time, I can go back to Moscow or Islamabad or Delhi. In Moscow, I would join the anti war protests and get thrown in jail with Navalny. I'd sneak in some food for him, from the American consulate, and make sure he wasn't being starved to death. But the Russians would take away the bread I was spooning to the best Putin dissident in the business, and probably put a bullet through his head, if they haven't already.

In Islamabad, I would change my name and have the fattiest, juiciest, richest lamb kabob over a bed of rice, and scour the open air markets in Karachi. But in Delhi–in Delhi–I wouldn't feast on food or join a political riot–I would first visit our old house in Vasant Vihar, but then look for traces of Keya everywhere in went: at the Red Fort I'd see her face etched in its turrets and bastions. I'd see her body at Humayun's tomb, smoothing its pillars, And when I'd see these things, I'd then hear her sing-sing voice calling to me late at night, in the ethers of blackness, when the moon was shining from the outskirt horizons of Mumbai or the tip-top slopes of Bangalore. Then, I would feel at peace with the world, even knowing that we were split apart–done with for good, a couple gone to the dust.

There are folks in other countries who I need to meet and sit down with. And folks up the eastern seaboard as well. Folks I need to split a martini with, or split a bottle of Cabernet, at a cafe somewhere in Paris or New York. And we need to have conversations–serious conversations about unfolded events. But until that day comes, and until those conversations are had, running away is the only thing I'd like to do. Run away from the fear, the anxiety, the looming, ominous, omnipresent monster that names some of my biggest demons. These demons are tricky to deal with, they eat at my core, and they rot my legs and arms away. None of them are my fault, and I never committed any serious wrong, but these demons exist nonetheless.

I have been in tricky situations before–at gunpoint, in a meat market in Tel Aviv, scrambling for my life, in the Bedouin desert, rife with racing thoughts and mania. And little I can do will stop some of these traumatic memories from bubbling to the surface–

from eclipsing me whole and swallowing me like a whale would to a minnow in the South Pacific.

Even though I'm dishing out most of the facts of my life religiously–too much, actually--other things go unspoken. Unsaid. And these are the things that are the most troubling–the devils doing backflips on your shoulders that no one can see–no one can pinpoint out of thin air. Only I know about the dark shadows that rip me to pieces, tear me apart on the inside, make silent suffering a thing again.

Suffering in silence is the worst kind of suffering imaginable. It is ominous. Scary. Frightening at every turn. Others don't recognize it. You are left to tatters, sleeping in a basement bed, sweating–again–in troves at night, into soaked shirts that you replace with more on the bedside stand. The suffering seems endless, like trauma is reaping through the mind and cutting it out into small, cookie cutter pieces.

Suffering in silence feels like a soldier is sticking a dagger through your kidney in broad daylight, and no one in any crowd passing by will notice the event. Suffering in silence feels like a madman is pouring gasoline over your head and lighting it on fire–also in broad daylight–while few others see what's going on. It is torture. Pain punctured through the skin. The worst part is not the suffering, but the silence, as the name implies. Not being able to name the pain. To voice it to others.

I am still the Runner-Away-In-Chief. There are simply too many things in this life that I just don't want to confront.

I don't want to go back to a place where I'm seeing and hearing things, Mom. It's not the real me. The real me is astute of my surroundings: a man of mystery able to navigate Jerusalem or Amman on foot. Able to go back to Delhi and prance through Visant Vihar dodging diplomatic plates. Able to serenade through Sochi and order a croissant in a remote town in Provence. Able to stumble drunkenly through an empty meat market in Tel Aviv and still make it alive to Jaffa.

When I'm well again the world will be my oyster: a parade of Irish bars and happy hour schmoozing and plane rides to Red Rocks. A realm of concerts and alcohol and more alcohol and the occasional bump of cocaine with ketamine. Cocaine with a K. Calvin Klein. But for the time being I make do with the Virginia countryside, with road trips to Queens and Princeton and Boston, where the public gardens call my name through lilies and fields of green.

When I'm well again the world will dissipate into a sea of clouds on top of a sea–a Caribbean sea I'll swim with a lover nearby. When I'm well again I'll have coffee in the fall to the tune of a hummingbird at 6am. When I'm well again I will get a job that pays more than 60,000, more than 80,000, more than 100,000. When I'm well again I will go to Harvard Business School and work on Wall Street. When I'm well again the monsters in my head will be shot down. When I'm well again the world will appear real to me: things I think will be true, and not false. When I'm well again I will make love to one thousand men and women. When I'm well again the pills in my cabinet will ebb day by day and I will finally drink low pulp orange juice at night. When I'm well again my head will be a blank canvas to draw thoughts on–not an impressionist painting full of shades of distorted black and gray.

When I'm well again the mania will be burned down by a flame. I won't be excited, won't be hyper, won't be crazed. When I'm well again, I'll be able to spend a night by myself in peace. When I'm well again I will take a man or woman back to my room without them questioning my sanity. When I'm well again I won't make myself bleed. When I'm well again I won't sweat through three shirts at night. When I'm well again I won't have to write this book just to get by.

But for now, I am not well, and I remain in Hurt Capital. My brain is soaking in the remnants of a year of mania. Delusions take over my day like firecrackers on the Fourth of July. Things come and go, but never stay. People mutter excuses to me. Family seems far. Friends appear as enemies, and enemies appear as friends. Daytime is an impressionist painting that I can't decipher. I can't tell what is right from wrong, true from fiction. The hours in my day don't make sense. The minutes don't make sense. The seconds tick by too slowly. Then when I get excited, they tick by quite fast. Time is an illusion. Reality is one too.

Do you know what is the biggest irony of them all? The least delusional thing about me is my gender. Conservatives might read this and say my transness is one big illusion–a story I concocted in my mind for the sake of telling a lie. Yet being a man is the thing in this world that grounds me the most–putting on a pair of Levi's, belting up, and shooting a gun at a range or in the forest. Wearing a gold chain around my neck like an Italian mobster. Bench pressing a hundred pounds. Calling another person a bro.

This is the thing that I want to run away from–the invisibility of it all. Maybe if I move to England, or France, and adopt a new ID, change names, change hair color, change face, maybe I can start over then. Begin a new chapter. A chapter of Isaac and not just Isabel. A chapter dedicated to nourishing others–feeding those I love, offering them the best drinks around town, getting rid of the bipolar. Maybe if I go to a hospital in some far flung region of Spain they can take all the mania away from the brain–all of the psychosis–all of the stuff I think is real but doesn't exist–and throw it into a trash bin. Maybe that can actually happen, Mom.

20

THAT DAY WILL never materialize. It won't happen. I know it, deep down, that this disease will stick with me for the rest of my life–perhaps for eternity, when I'm either sitting in heaven or hell waiting to get judged by God. Even then, God will spring mania on me.

The mind is never satisfied, never.

The mind is never satisfied, never. ed, never.

It's Christmas Eve, but for the first time feels like Santa isn't going to come. Not this year. Twenty nine was a harsh awakening to the world—too harsh. People around me are dying. Rick Olson, our family friend, has stage 4 prostrate cancer. He was hunted by the FBI for a bit and he thinks the stress of that led him to be so sick. I remember hikes with Rick at Great Falls, and a Thanksgiving dinner with his then-wife.

Rashmi was also passing, and passed. When I go back to her house I feel her presence looming over me like a storm about to break. The rains will be harsh, and her voice will whisper down my ear: *take care. Take care, Isaac!*

Other people around me are dying—young people, people who shouldn't be this sick. People who deserve wealth and prosperity but are instead making trips up to Johns Hopkins. By themself.

The greatest tragedy in life is not death in general but rather death in people who don't deserve it. A long time ago you let me meet Suleiman Bakhit. You were ambassador in Jordan, and Suleiman was the son of the former prime minister. He was crafting comic books to defeat ISIS propaganda. Through his pictures and letters, Suleiman was teaching young people not to join extremist groups.

Suleiman was brave over coffee. We spoke for a few hours, and he told the stories of men in the Arab world who were ashamed of their sexuality. I was ashamed too—back at the time—when I sported a short haircut and was a lesbian, Suleiman didn't laugh at me or look the other way. He proudly welcomed me into his world.

But Suleiman was sick too, Mom. He had brain cancer, and it wasn't getting any better. He passed at the age of 40. Out of all the people I've known, he didn't deserve to die the most. He was a soldier. We're all soldiers in different ways, Mom. You're a soldier too, because of all the misogynistic shit you've had to put up with in the workplace. Dodging piggish men who want to see you fail.

I'm a solider for changing my gender and living with bipolar. Every day I'm awake feels like a new rising in the war field: a new battle to wage in my mind and body, and a new battle to wage with people—making sure I won't be called a tranny the next day and avoiding punches at the bar. Making sure the meds work. Making sure I can live and breathe to see another day with you and Dad walking around the sun. With Helen powering through the workplace. With friends nearby.

But people are dying. Some are dying slowly, while others are dying fast. And it's not fair—not fair at all. They're going too soon. Up, away, and into the horizon, tucked into some pocket of heaven where the sun's golden rays can bounce back and forth, offering them light. And once again—not one bit of it is fair.

21

GIULIO IS GROWING up. I finally got him on the dating apps. He's on Tinder, Hinge, and Bumble. I fixed up all of his pictures and everything. So he has a stache in one and muscles in the next. Now he's getting texts from this Swedish girl, and I think they're talking back and forth and I–I swear to–I swear to God–I hope he gets laid.

I talk to Giulio about sexuality. I say I like both dudes and women, and he's okay with that.

The bipolar has gotten better. I'm feeling better, acting better–not wanting to get into these fist fights with monstrous men at the bar. But I probably should. Something in my mind has cleared–a maelstrom of sorts, a shitstorm that was brewing up for a while. I barely get hypomanic too, as well, which is a fucking miracle, Mom.

You know, Mom, despite all of my talk and delusions and mania, I will find a way to succeed in spite of this book. This book is career suicide, but I'm a smart enough man to figure it out.

There is an entrepreneurial spirit that lives in me–one that wants to create new companies, and not destroy them from within. One that wants to build a castle of an enterprise, and not clock my 9 to 5 at any old firm.

I am at Nanny O'brien's again. The men that stew here are, indeed, slightly monstrous, and I try to avoid them at all costs. They are creepy, lewd drunkards. Yet I do find that coming here is an exemplary exercise in conversation–in tactics–in avoiding one man from groping me and telling another one about my grandma at the same time.

Past midnight, all bets are off. The drunkards might want to rape or pillage, or they might want to gift me a million dollars when they're too tipsy. You just have no idea. It's best sometimes to stick to your phone and type this book out while the entire world catches on fire.

Being at this bar is the perfect exercise in dodging shady people and shitty characters. I imagine you have had to do this a lot as a female diplomat–as a woman going to bases in Saudi Arabia and flying to Kabul, as a blonde-haired and blue-eyed mother who has to talk to the Taliban.

I wonder what the Taliban thought of you. I wondered if they wanted to marry you, or kill you, or hit you, or kidnap you into the Hindu Kush. I wonder if some of the warlords have ever wanted to gift you anything, or court you, or throw you off a cliff, or just simply make a deal with you to make their life better.

Perhaps they thought you were trendy, with a chic outfit, or perhaps they thought you were irritating, with an American accent and high heels. Maybe they thought you were a threat. A nuisance. A dangerous missile gone rogue. Maybe they thought you were just good at your job, or maybe they hated you. Maybe it was a mixture of both.

I'm still thinking about Giulio. I want him to become a man, just like I became one, on my own accord, as well.

22

THE PILLS IN the bathroom cabinet are not athletes this time, but artists. And to be specific, they are *writers,* Mom. But only the best writers, in a somewhat put together order of importance: Morrison, Dostoevsky, Camus, Hemingway, Zadie Smith. Pushkin and T.S. Eliot as well. They are moving their godforsaken pens–and their godforsaken typewriters–to make magic happen.

The Wasteland will save me from eternal mania. *Crime and Punishment* is going to be good for my brain, and Raskolnikov is working in my favor–he more deranged than I. *The Stranger* is rooting for me as well, and it's the best antidote to bipolar–is reading Camus' lines. And last, but certainly not least, *Song of Solomon* is protecting bipolar as well–it is shielding me from the worst depressive state known to man.

Despite what you've given me, despite your charm with the Taliban, despite your smarts and embrace, I think about fleeing to Boston sometimes, or the Virgin Islands, or Cancun. In these fantasies–in Boston–I would work at Harvard's library, and write this book while doing it. I would work under the guidance of a famous, world class professor–maybe one who won a Pulitzer, just like my old guy Michael Cunningham did.

In the Virgin Islands, in Saint Thomas, I would serve drinks at a tiki bar and flirt with beautiful women.

Mom, when you die, I'm going to name an International Foundation after you. It's going to be headquartered in DC–in Georgetown–and it's going to be named the Alice W. Wells Institute for Diplomacy. With this Institute, I will invite top diplomats across the world to its halls. The Kazakhs love you–they always have, and always will. I'm going to invite some Uzbeks as well. And some Russians at that–let's just throw some Russians in there for fun. Then what I'm going to do is–what I'm going to do is this–I'm going to take a group of around twenty men, maybe nineteen, maybe twenty-two, and I'm going to seat them all at a round table, next to a hall of flags.

At this table, I will give a Powerpoint presentation to these men, and the powerpoint will explain, in vivid detail, how shitty they are as diplomats compared to you. I'm going to take note of their careers, and I'm going to highlight notes from their negotiations with other nations–maybe France, maybe England, maybe Germany. Maybe some Netherlands at that. And I'm going to compare their negotiations to yours–to your negotiations with the Taliban. And I'm going to do this because I'll have FOIA'd your records with the Taliban.

All of your records will be FOAI'd, Mom, and I'm going to tell these diplomats that they are awful at their job. That *you* were the best. The only one who did it right in the whole damn business, if you ask me.

The bipolar is killing me, Mom, slowly, day by day. It's taking inventory of my brain and destroying it as it chooses–seeing neural pathways as things to cripple, and not enliven. My disease doesn't care about me–in fact, it actively hates me and wants me dead. It is a soldier I can't control, a missile gone astray. I don't have Iron Dome to protect against it. Hamas is going to rain bombs on Tel Aviv and Tel Aviv can't defend itself. Just like my brain can't defend itself either. Give me something to survive. GIve me a better med, better sleep, better doctors. Give me anything and I'll lose track of time, turning sad mornings into happy days. I want to thumb through the pages of a paperback again and feel surprised: surprised at their incandescent smell, surprised at the weight they put on my index fingers. I want to laugh at a cafe in Dupont Circle. I want to kiss a new lover on the neck. I want many things, but none are coming true.

Mom, I have witnessed the most miserable days. I have seen darkness that you can't even picture in the blackest shades. The bipolar has wrecked my mind in ways I can't articulate. Ways I can't describe. Ways I can't put into words. The disease is a blanket that wraps itself around my body and controls it into half-cut limbs. It tears my heart into bloody remnants of choked arteries. It swallows me whole.

Your ambassadorship isn't going to save me. No amount of talks with the Taliban will stop me from thinking things that aren't true. Sometimes I wish they would, though. There's a clip of you in the New York Times (name newspaper). Sometimes I wish the Taliban was my bipolar, and you were negotiating its release.

Cooking is my form of meditation now. Sitting still for endless minutes and trying to focus on the present just makes me space out even more. So instead of doing that, I've found solace in chopping meat and sauteing vegetables. Tonight's menu item was pork ragu. It's a Friday, and I have no friends to see–no lover to dote on. No pet to take care of. Just a bachelor and his knives.

Perfect for the winter, ragu boasts a warm taste and rich texture, with braised pig shoulders that slide off an invisible bone into a concoction of tomatoes and rosemary and carrots. The pasta used is tagliatelle–Wegman's ran out of pappardelle–but the key is to keep it an egg pasta, which it is, and make sure that the strains are somewhat wide and long. Egg pastas do better with holding up the weight of thick and tender pork.

And bam! As the rosemary hits the Dutch oven it will cure mania forever, Mom. Cure it forever. I chop the vegetables beforehand–diligently–astutely–until they are diced into fine cubes, the celery and carrots and onions. Once everything is in there–including garlic and thyme and sage–the medley goes round and round for a bit, until there are brown bits left at the bottom of the pan. *Then* it is time for red wine, Mom. I get a dry wine–Cabernet–and make sure the top is twist off, because who wants to spend extra minutes corkscrewing cooking wine? One cup of Cabernet goes onto the Dutch oven, and this is to deglaze everything–deglaze the residue from vegetables overheating. But as the red wine also hits the bottom of the pan, I think of ways in which this recipe could cure me of the bipolar. Maybe it can calm me down a bit, take me back to the present moment, and not one in which my mind is plagued by trauma.

Now the pork shoulders come in. I got a fat two pound draw of boneless pork shoulder, which got cut up into four chunks. I browned the chunks a bit beforehand, then set them aside on the plate. After emptying an entire can of whole tomatoes into the vegetable and wine mix, the pork comes. The tomatoes I beat up raw and sliced in pieces with the tail end of my wooden spoon. But let's not forget that the pork has made a glorious appearance. And now I'm thinking that this pork can defend me from everything on this Earth–including psychosis and the rollercoaster ride of mood swings. The pork, which will transform into tender, sweet meat, will cure me of all depression in the future. The pork is a soldier, Mom. It is a shield against all that is bad in the world. And the world is one hell of a bad place, Mama.

I close the lid to the Dutch oven and place it in the stove. Two hours will go by until the meat sauce is ready. On the burners, I place a big pot of salted water next to the tagliatelle. In ninety minutes it will be ready to go. Nina Simone comes on the stereo–this is *I Wish I Knew How It Would Feel To Be Free.* She's crooning live from a stage in Baltimore, and playing the piano as the seconds tick by. *She* didn't know what it was like to be fully free. *I* don't know what it is like to be fully free, but boy I wish I did, Mama.

When I feel like not running away–like sitting still–I'm calm again, stable, seduced by doing the same things and seeing the same people. But there are still people–and let me repeat this–there are still people in far flung cities overseas and up the Eastern seaboard who I need to have difficult conversations with. When I say difficult, I mean the hardest conversations one can imagine–ones involving death, the meaning of life, and mistakes. I'm scared of these conversations. Coming out as trans and realizing I was bipolar at the same time pale in comparison to the toughness of these new talks I need to have–these talks that will ease my conscience and put me back to sleep at night.

I have a friend–a graphic designer–who I'm worried is going to be homeless soon. He has no care for what roof is over his head–or for the fact that there is one over his head to begin with. Secretly, I think he has bipolar. I think he has broken himself off from reality and is in the pits, but pretends like he isn't. I'm doing everything in my power–everything in his best interest–to keep him in housing, to keep him winning design projects, to keep him fed and medicated. But I don't think he wants to be medicated, or even knows what that means.

It sounds ominous, but really isn't. Self-care means doing hard things–not easy ones. Self care is more than just bubble baths, massages, Whole Foods, therapy, and yoga. It is confronting the things in life that make you want to run away. And I promise you Mama–I promise you–that I will have these conversations one day, some abroad, others at home. And I promise you that I won't run away.

This is the crux of the matter: this is why I'm writing this book to begin with, to talk about these challenges. And I want to be as open as possible with you, and with the world, and there will be a price to pay–there will be a steep price to pay when conservatives and bigots and close minded people read these pages. They will say all sorts of things, and these things–after all I have been through–the backlash I might get from this book might drive me to borderline suicidality, but I'm okay with that, as long as the world knows my truth. Or at least 90% of it.

I'm going to have a difficult conversation with a bottle of Cabernet or Bordeaux, stocked right from France, from the southern region of that wine-loving country. I'm going to open the bottle myself–not with a hammer and nail–but with a corkscrew, and I'm going to pour two glasses, maybe three, depending on the parties involved. And we're going to talk. Talk things out, like true gentlemen–like men upholding the common good. Eventually, we'll reach a consensus, and retire for the night–in some godforsaken hostel in Europe or in my home territory, maybe in Queens, New York, or in DC itself. I'm a King of DC, by the way, just so you know that–I'm a King of DC.

The most difficult part of life for me, right now, is not being trans, or bipolar, but thinking about what I would do if I got sick, when I am still young–just like Suleiman Bakhit did. Just like some of my other friends are sick. And the question of death–the question of death in young ones is one I haven't answered yet, and

I've answered many, many questions before in my head, and I've deliberated hard things, and come to conclusions. But perhaps the only question that haunts my brain, besides the notion that I can become truly crazy some day–not just a bit crazy, but fully insane–and spend the rest of my life in a psych ward like McLean. I worry less about the latter, but more about the former.

I come out to the country three days a week now. The house being inhabited by no one else, the country offers a space to reflect and move on in life. The pastures call names out at dawn and dusk, and the rolling mountains of the Shenandoah are nearby. Somehow, I feel like I'm in the South: like this is Virginia's version of the South, and in the South, everything is done slow, and everything is done for comfort. Indeed, it's comfortable here, without having to worry about the hustle and bustle of DC. The district brims to the rim with go-getters–politicians and lobbyists and lawyers and businessmen just fiending for some more money, more meetings with the president, more trips to Capitol Hill. People out here, out in Sperryville, just care about one thing and one thing only: the state of their farm. If the farm is doing well–if the crops are growing, if the bees are making honey, if the orchards are blooming apples on time. And then they care about their friends, and their family, but mainly just the farms, Mom.

THE SKIES ARE CLEAR today.

Bipolar's middle name is Self-Sabotage: self-sabotaging relationships, jobs, nutrition, substance use, and all sorts of other things. The key to defeating bipolar, silently, step by step–besides taking meds and doing therapy–is to slowly train your brian to *not* sabotage everything, and to focus on self-preservation.

What does self-preservation mean? It means many things, Mom. At its core, self preservation means sustaining things–sustaining friendships and relationships and physical health. And mental health, of course. Self preservation means that when you feel any incoming mania, and know you will take it out on your friends, to actually skip that bar appointment you had with Curt or Keya.

Self-preservation means not skipping lithium doses. Tons of patients skip lithium because it makes them as miserable as can be–it dims your world, day by day, so you live in an empty shell of misery and sadness, as opposed to loitering in the cacophony of joy and elation that mania offers. But it's important to choose to be *miserable* and well as opposed to psychotically confident and unwell.

Self-preservation means handing my twin sister the keys to my bank account if I become manic again, so I don't blow thousands on tattoos or rowing machines or concert tickets and flights to unknown destinations.

Self-preservation means not taking out any kind of depression on a spouse or partner. It means closing the door to your bedroom and wallowing away for a few hours as the anger subsides. Instead of the anger taking full control of you–letting it wave your fingers are passerby, insult strangers, and break things on the ground.

Self-preservation means exercising the hypomania out of your body–weight by weight, shoulder rep by shoulder rep, benchpress by benchpress. The energy willowing away underneath the skin will slowly dissipate through sweat and blistered hands, and it will–and I promise you–it will go away, eventually, after minutes, hours, and just a few days.

Self-preservation means watching your words carefully–not *too* carefully, but carefully enough to not make a verbal mistake–to not call–god forbid–someone a cunt, or a *motherfucker*, or a bastard who has no job. Self preservation means having safe sex–it can still be great sex–but it has to be safe.

Self-preservation means going to the gym three times a week and finally buying those nicotine patches to wear instead of hitting the godforsaken vape. Self preservation means drinking three non alcoholic beers and two real Heinekens, instead of downing an entire Heineken six pack.

Self-preservation means going to bed at nine. Ten. Eleven. And waking up at eight with the rest of working America. Self preservation means coaching yourself to not feel the urge to down two pill bottles to let go of life. Self preservation means practicing a healthy mindset–one in which you can see the world as an oyster that approves of trans people, instead of the opposite.

Self-preservation means choosing the right kind of people to be around–the kind of people who don't mind a book like *Hurt Capital* coming out, who don't mind chatter of lithium tests and psychiatric visits. Self preservation means choosing these people–mostly artists and vagabonds and rogue creatives–to stick around, instead of leave. And *saying* things and doing things to make them feel appreciated.

Self-preservation means choosing the right job, too, and the right grad program–and the job has to line up with your values, if you can make that be.

Self-sabotage needs to go away, Mom. It needs to go away forever. It needs to disappear into the distance, a faint memory never to be traced again. But self preservation is here to stay.

23

In my mind, I am taken to a place where things are at peace again. We are back in Delhi, and a Gandhi statue is peering at us nearby. We go to Delhi Haat and rummage for books, and you buy us Lays chips. We are in Agra, and it is hot–scorching hot–but all that matters is the touch of ice cold water to the lips, and the Taj Mahal. We take off our shoes before entering and go to the back of the monument–where there's stairs–and the Yuma river sits right there, a barren wasteland laying way to another village. Helen, Phoebe and I play on the steps, careless–just adventurers in a wondrous world. Then my mind takes me back to Islamabad–to Pakistan–before India ever happened. In these memories, we're at a ski resort in the mountains, and we've driven through Abbottabad, where bin Laden would eventually hide. It's not winter, but the altitude gives us some fresh air and height above the looming cities below. Then we venture into Karachi, which is the New York City of Pakistan–crowded, bustling with vendors, every item on sale in open air markets. We buy a remnant of a necklace, or something like that. Back in India, years later, you gift us little Ganesh statues–one of which I keep near my bed.

In these days, the bipolar doesn't exist and the world's evils don't show up on a doorstep. The cruelty of the world is minimized by you: a guardian and protector. Even back then–back in those days–you seemed smarter than other mothers, and a bit brilliant too. You seemed different–like you carried a different intellect in your head. In these days, gender didn't exist yet–neither male nor female held any sway in life, any weight on anything. No one is really gendered, including myself. Money doesn't exist yet, except for a few Rupees to buy soda, and I don't have to worry about carrying on a family legacy, entering corporate America and making sure we thrive into future generations. I haven't been made fun of by dozens and dozens of people, and I don't have to worry about seeing spiders barreling at me or hearing cop sirens.

These were the days of peace, Mom. Now the world has been turned upside down, and contorted into weird shapes. Reality often doesn't make sense, and I don't see all of it. I can't decipher what is true from untrue, what is right from not right. Many months are spent trying to stay alive: trying to avoid suicide, or any kind of hallucinations, and any kind of mania. I'm trying to avoid psychosis at all costs. So I throw myself into work: into the GRE, into poetry, into writing columns and being on a statewide board.

The world will never go back to what it used to be–no matter how hard I try, this reality can never return to the days of India and Pakistan, where the environment around us was bustling with chaos, but insi–inside my mind–everything was at peace. How ironic, that things were the most calm in the busiest, most hectic of places.

I try to recreate India and Pakistan in the world outside of me, when I visit New York and go to Jackson Heights, in Queens. There, at least, is a little mini India, full of dosas and japati and all sorts of curry. The sights in Jackson Heights are dizzying–the lights technicolor at night, the vendors screaming at the top of their lungs, sometimes, and the passerby fiending for the best *chaat*. Nothing is perfect, and I will always carry a psychiatric history–but I didn't carry a psychiatric history living in South Asia, so I pretend I don't have the bipolar in Jackson Heights. It's refreshing, really, to pretend like chaos doesn't exist–like madness is not around the corner–like insanity doesn't constantly loom on a far horizon.

So Jackson Heights is a safe space–a refuge of sorts–an atmosphere where I can nourish and cultivate, as opposed to destroy and self sabotage. Jackson Heights is where my heart lies, and South Asia is where my mind was at peace.

THE HALLMARK OF BEING trans in the 21st century is feeling lesser than. Lesser than everyone, Mom. The other guys at the gym have been guys their entire life, and walk around with built biceps and massive chests, tall frames and thick legs, if they so choose. They carry these dumb gym bags, and walk around with protein shakes, and when it is their turn, they can easily benchpress two hundred pounds, without trying, because they've had testosterone in their body since day one. These guys might get naked pictures from girls, and then they'll circulate them to *more* guys, and their high school friend group will laugh. When these so-called men go home at night, they can get laid with another straight, cis girl in a heartbeat, because that girl is looking for their prototype of man. These people make me feel lesser than.

When I go back to a college campus, I see sorority girls going to a party. I know, deep down, that most of these sorority girls wouldn't sleep with me, but that's okay–because it's their right to choose. I haven't earned any bed time. But I know that a lot of these sorority girls would also choose not to be close friends with me–they may feign interest, or mock as an acquaintance, but they are more content traveling in their wealthy, cis-inhabited, straight-dominant world. They'd rather not deal with the burden and pressure and weirdness of being close to a trans guy.

At a career fair, I see professionals who have been the same person their entire life. They grew up in the same town. Went to a state college or an Ivy. Stayed friends with the same people from high school *and* college. They never had to change their name, change their pronouns, change the way they dressed and looked–and changed their personality. They never had to alter their life, they rarely had to deal with friends cutting them off, and they never fluctuated that much in weight, or had to quit a sports team because they hated it so much, or wrote articles that were so provocative they got insulted in emails. These people never had to defend their gender to transphobes. They never had to avoid bar fights because of the sex they weren't born with. They never had to be cautious while dating–never had to be afraid of rape just because of the genitals in their pants. They never had to realize that the twin they grew up with since birth wasn't a spitting image of them anymore. They never had to push their body so hard to conform to a workplace standard–one in which everyone should look cis. These people don't know what it's like to struggle in these ways. But I do. I do, Mama. And these people make me feel lesser than.

In any given workplace, there are men and women who are conservative–who have voted Republican. These men and women may have been in the army, or the navy, or maybe they're just plain old engineers. These men and women could have gone to many Virginia Tech football games, or Redskins games, or Wizards games. They enjoy watching sports all day and drinking beer. They don't read literature. They don't like plays. They've forgotten who Shakespeare was, and they certainly don't know about Hemingway. These people likely have two kids and a golden retriever in a suburb–in a house with a white fence. Both spouses are straight, and they earn low six figures. Together, they can afford one two week trip to Disney each year. They might even bring their dog. Whether they know it or not, these people also might not like to have trans friends in their lives. We just fuck things up–we alter their worldview in a way that they don't want to see it change. We mess with their lifestyle. With their beliefs. We are counter culture, and we think that trans people should be in sports. But they don't. They don't think we should be in sports one bit, Mom. *These* people make me feel lesser than. And they make other trans people feel lesser than as well, Mom. I would rather get shot by ISIS than have to socialize with these folk.

I max out on reading Tolstoy and Pushkin. Our *cat* is named Pushkin. When I was 17, back in high school—back in high school—before I was of legal age, I got a tattoo of wings on my ankle because our English class read *Song of Solomon. Song of Solomon*, Mama. And the quote that inspired the wings was "wanna fly, gotta give up the shit that weighs you down". The shit that weighs you down! There is a lot of shit that weighs me down. But not you.

Recently, I've tattooed the words "AMOR VINCIT OMNIA" on my chest. And there is an AB tattoo on my back. AB stands for Anthony Bourdain. Amor Vincit Omnia means that love conquers all. In Latin. And it's in my first poetry book—*Amor Vincit Omnia* is etched into my first book. Because the entire premise is—well, the premise of the matter is that as long as you can love and are loved in return, then nothing in life can seriously weigh you down. Love makes the world go around, and it lifts us up in the darkest of times—when when Jews were enslaved at Auschwitz, in times when real people were slaves in the South, in times when trans people were demonized at Stonewall. In times when gays were denied the right to marry, in times when Trump stole our freedom while proclaiming to wave it in a flag. In times when *you* cried because Dad was in Afghanistan, in times when *Dad* might have cried because he was in Afghanistan himself. In times when I cry because of the bipolar, in times when Helen cries because of anxiety. In times when a single mom can't get a food stamp, in times when a homeless man has to amputate an arm. In times when drug dealers are thrown into jail and left to fiend to murderers and rapists. In times when women are raped, when men are raped. In times when my mind is raped by mania. This is when love matters the most, Mom. And you have loved me in spite of all of these troubles.

Love conquers all. Love indeed conquers all. I've fallen in love with four women over the course of my lifetime, and briefly might have been in love with a man, for one instant—just one instant at a cafe. But the majority of these people were women. And they made me feel fierce on the inside—like I could conquer my mania and psychosis like none other. These women made me feel like a soldier, and like they loved me like I was a fighter—fighting this disease of the mind one pill at a time, one doctor's visit at a time. Even when my brain was full of trauma. Full of crazed energy. Full of nonsense. These women made me feel special. And they made my *words* feel special—like adjectives that just had seen the light of day, like verbs that carry a sword and shield as they dot their *I*s and cross their *T*s. These women lifted me up like none other, and made me feel worthy to be a king.

24

LITERATURE IS THE key to the universe. Hemingway did a good job, but Morrison did an even better one. And Zadie Smith sure as hell knows how to write. The best literature should be subversive–the kind that makes someone uncomfortable.

The world is saved by literature. It's not made better by math, or science, or history. Literature, instead, is what makes the sun shine–what makes the moon full of light at night. Literature is why the stars are sprinkled across the sky, it's why a girl will kiss me, softly, on the lips. It's why you love me. It's why I love *you.*

Literature is how the bipolar will be cured–through line after line of prose, of writing satanic and angelic verses, of spooning feelings out on paper like they are gems waiting to be examined–jealousy revealed, anger uncovered, depression unveiled.

Dostoevsky is what makes the Earth turn at night. Camus is what puts us to sleep. James Baldwin is screaming from the forest at the top of his lungs, telling us to move to France, and to stop being so damn racist. Zadie Smith is perched somewhere in New York City, writing the best novel known to man. Authors both dead and alive make the planet turn on its axis. We are the heroes. The antiheroes, even. The saviors and charlatans and renaissance men of life. We are artists, Mom. Artists at our very core.

Do you know what literary OCD is? I do. It's when you buy four copies of *Song of Solomon* from Amazon and put one on the bedroom drawer, another in the kitchen, and one in the car. The fourth copy is meant to be with you at all times: when you go to the bathroom at an Irish bar, when you are making love to someone in a foreign apartment, and when you are at the zoo. Staring at lions, a copy of *Song of Solomon* will be clasped into your hands, with nowhere to go. It won't move. It won't budge. It'll just stay there, and calm the mind. Just knowing that the book is next to me puts me at ease. Knowing that its characters and soul pervades the air around me makes my breathing slower, heart rate more normal. It makes me feel relaxed again. Things are smoother. Easier when that book is around.

Milkman is the main character in the novel. I don't think he was a good guy, Mom. I really don't. The entire book is about how he finds himself. His identity in his family: there is a pot of gold involved and some insurance man flies off of a building. But I really think the insurance man wanted to kill himself. But I'm not really sure what happened there. Toni Morrison has a way with playing with words–with making magic happen, if you ask me. And that's why I'm here writing to you, and that's why I'm here with literary OCD, because I need that goddamn book next to me at all times.

I don't think Milkman was a good guy. I really don't think he was, Mom. I know he was trying to find himself, but just something *about* him rubs me the wrong way. I think he was too self-possessed, too self-contained, too obsessed with himself. Too narcissistic. I don't think he cared enough about others.

THE FIRST HALLMARK OF a creative genius is constant daydreaming. I go to Trader Joe's. The frozen pork shumai dumplings lay barren there, still, waiting to be snatched for sale. A movie starts to play through my mind: the girl of my dreams, a Russian heiress, is eating these pork dumplings with me, at a table in Moscow. We're talking about Tolstoy, and Dostoevsky, and Pushkin–all of these dead men. She bends over the table and places a kiss on my right cheek. Her lipstick dissipates into my skin. It's red, and makes me warm. The next item I buy at Trader Joe's are bananas. They're fresh, and from Ecuador. Now I'm in Quito, eating bananas to my heart's content. Julio Jaramillo is playing on a radio in a misshapen bar. *Misshapen* is another word plucked from my hidden dictionary. The banana leaves my palette wanting more.

Kanye is a creative genius. Elon Musk is a creative genius. John Williams, who made the score to Harry Potter, is a creative genius. Creative geniuses do a second thing: we become fiercely, willfully, powerfully independent. The most toxic thing to do to a creative genius is place them in a group. They will have to conform, and be bossed around, and take orders. It isn't fun. Isn't fun at all, Mom.

Because creative geniuses are so independent, people see us as weird. Strange. Beyond the pale. Some of our actions don't make sense, and sometimes what we say doesn't make any sense either. We are inherently nonsensical, at best. We operate differently. We are primarily Renaissance Creatures, beholden to study dozens of topics at once. *Real estate. Law. Calculus. Fiction. Poetry. Calculus.* Our minds twist and turn in ways mysterious to the general public. We might have outbursts, but these outbursts only happen because we don't know how to channel our energy elsewhere. When we do channel our energy appropriately, we make wondrous art. Art that shocks and stuns the world. Art that will change your life forever.

Some writers are social pariahs. We are not in the crowd. We stand out like sore thumbs, yet find ways to still fit in. *Drink beer. Watch basketball. Play in a soccer league. Joke about sex.* These are just mechanisms—just currencies—for not being outed as strange, a dilapidated house ridden with all sorts of weird crevices and 70 degree angles. For not being outed as outlandish, aberrant—and aber—aberrant is another word from the hidden dictionary. Ah. Webster says it means "departing from an accepted standard". So I was right, after all.

Really good writers are often broken people. Hemingway almost drank himself to death and then shot his head. Sylvia Plath committed suicide. And David Foster Wallace hung himself from his back porch.

Mom, I don't belong on this Earth. *You* do. You've got all the smarts about you. You're intelligent. You have blonde hair. You've spoken Russian and Arabic. You were courted by a Saudi prince when you were in Riyadh. You know diplomacy. You've bargained with the Taliban in Doha. You know your place in the world.

I don't. I'm wretched—a monster beholden to the saddest nightmares. My religion is alcohol, and my cross is a pint of Heineken. Jesus is the owner of Coors Light. Mary is the bartender next door.

Talk about how I'm not street smart.

Mom, my entire adult life I've been running away from one thing. Not my transness. Not my bipolar. Not any of that. Just one thing that I can't tell anyone about.

I AM AT A pub now. It is an Irish joint, sneaked into Cleveland Park. Nanny O'Briens. *Nanny O'Briens.* Just saying that name makes me feel good. I meet the dirties of men here–men who are worse than Milkman. Men who try to touch my body when I tell them I might be gay, even when I'm not. Men who want to get into fights. But I also meet men who have stories short and tall to tell–I meet musicians who string the violin to Irish music and grandfathers who miss their nephews.

We watch Travis Kelce play the Lions–and speaking of Travis Kelce–he is a linebacker, and the pills in my medicine cabinet are linebackers too. And they're doing pretty well, if you ask me. And *I'm* doing well Mom. I'm doing better, ever since rehab, ever since doing all of those godforsaken benzos to feel better. I'm much healthier now, and now is the ti–now is the time to find a beautiful and smart woman, just like you. I have a few heiresses in mind. These heresses have probably been on yachts in the Mediterranean, and they have probably spoken to Russian oligarchs–just as I almost have in Moscow.

I just sat next to a famous Democrat at the bar, and he was creepy. He's deaf. A former legal counsel to Nancy Pelosi. And he just kept touching me, even after I told him to stop touching. Democrats can be creepy, Mom. They can be rude. They can rape. Just like Bill Clinton did. I'm now even more convinced that political party is as good a litmus test for character as temperature is a test for a city in the throes of climate change. I'm sick of being a semi prominent Democrat in DC because it means I get exposed to the worst Democrats around. And let me tell you who the worst Democrats are: they are the Democrats at the very top, the Democrats who seek power and backstab each other. Like the Democrat who just touched me too much. Like Democrats who slander each other. I was once hired by a Democrat to send another one to jail. I'm not even making that up Mom. I declined the job. Being a Democrat so much has made me want to be Republica now. But I bet the Republicans do the same shit, and just even more. Maybe there is something wrong with the people who seek power: maybe the more power one seeks, the worse they are as a person. I'm sick of this stuff. Fuck the Democratic Party. Snakes exist in all shapes, sizes, and voting records. They exist no matter what. Maybe politics is a bad game to play, Mama.

25

LET ME TELL you why Toni Morrison is the best author of all time. Now just to be clear, Morrison is better than the top ten white, dead, male authors ever: Shakespeare, Camus, Hemingway, etc. She's better than all ten of them combined. She far surpasses them at every road turn. There are four reasons for why she's so great.

First, her vocabulary is unrivaled. As a child, Morrison ate up her local library–she basically read every book there. So some of the words she uses seem very magical and complex in nature–words most people have never heard of.

Second, she's the first award-winning author to only use black people in her books. In only writing about African American characters, she's flipping the damn script on the oppressor. She's making white people feel like they're the minority. One of these days, Mom–one of these days–I'm going to write a book with only trans people in it. Well, there might be one cis person–only one–and they might be a household servant, or a slave.

The third reason why Toni is the best author is she has always treasured wisdom in writing and in people. I've watched every single interview with her, and she particularly cherished how wise President Obama was compared to other past candidates. There's much wisdom in her writing, Mama. The epigraph to "*Song of*

Solomon" is "the fathers may soar/ And the children may know their names." That's pretty profound, Mom. Lastly, Toni uses magical realism, which basically means she creates two fictional constructs in one book. The first fictional construct is to set up the plot and setting of the novel, but she adds a second layer of fiction to that by creating scenes and people in the novel that do not make sense, and are magical. That's very difficult to do.

Mom, when I was manic for one year I got a tattoo of *Song of Solomon* on my left bicep. I was so manic that I thought it was going to look good, and now it doesn't. It's ugly, and I get made fun of a lot for it. But I don't care. I don't give a damn. One of these days, I might hire someone to turn the tattoo in a nice, big floral sleeve–full of irises and roses and peachy vines. But until then, I love what's on my arm, and I'll love Toni forever.

I saw Morrison, in 2015, at Harvard, with a girl from my high school cross country team. I believe Morrison was in a wheelchair, and she was sick Mom–I think she could have been sick back then. I'm not sure. Either way, Morrison would pop up in my dreams from time to time, and to tell you the tru–to tell you the truth–in my dreams I showed up at her office in Princeton, and she just shooed me away, calling me an annoying white boy.

But boy, Mama, if I was at Princeton at the time, I would have fought tooth and nail to get into Toni's damn class. And then I would have produced the finest work of fiction for her–so fine it would almost rival *Song of Solomon*–but then it would stop short at that, and recede into the abyss. Her pages would conquer mine, and her vocabulary would be better. And all of her little plots–well all of her little plot lines would be thicker than mine, and better, and I would just look like a goddamn fool in front of her. But I would love her nonetheless. That I am sure of, Mom. That I am sure as hell sure of.

Actually, there is a woman in New Haven whom I greatly admire. She, just like me, likes reading Toni Morrison. Actually, she does close readings of Morrison and teaches her in classes. If she is at all willing to talk, I would like to extend an invitation for drinks to her for all of the help she proffered me at Yale. But that's only if she wants to talk.

How did she do it, Mom? How did Morrison get away with slaughtering the entire literary establishment to pieces? My second church is literature, and Morrison is the God. There's no other way to say it. Everyone needs to worship her books. *Song of Solomon. Sula. Beloved.* Morrison is a deity, and we are all just peasants. Her words rule over mine. They conquer my land.

THE ONLY THING SAVING me from wanting to put a bullet in my head is lite--literature. And that's because I'm brill–I'm brilliant, Mama, and writing books is what saves the whole goddamn world, if you ask me. And if you really want to know the truth, nothing in this life matters except for family, friends, and good, good, good ass literature. GAL. *Literature.* The end all be all of the Earth. The best craft known to man. These stories–stories of Raskolnikov and Holden Caulfield and Iago–these stories are passed down through years, decades, centuries. They suffer through occasional book burnings but then come back to life. And *writing* these godforsaken stories is what makes the world go round. It's what sets the moon on fire–shining so bright a lunar eclipse can illuminate the darkest of woods, the loneliest of animals, the hermetic authors living solitarily like JD Salinger once did, a long time ago. After he came out with *Catcher in the Rye.*

I AM SICK OF people, Mom. People are the source of all world issues–not global warming, not polar bears in the Arctic, not lower taxes. It's people who make others feel miserable, sick on the inside, and not willing to get out of the house.

I've always had a mixed track record with people. At Yale, the women's rugby kicked me off their team, for no apparent reason perhaps other than the fact that I was transitioning into a man who liked to wear Marines shirts and weight lift with a protein shake in hand.

Do you know how much shit I've gotten from others? It's unbearable, Mom. Makes me want to retire back to my bed and sleep the day away, forgetting that the world even existed to begin with.

But the person who has treated me with the most kindness in this world is Keya. With black hair, dark eyes, and a skinny frame, Keya can save anyone. Her love was coming from a well that would never go dry–she adored me like none other. And I do miss her, Mom. Every day of the year, and most waking hours of the day as well.

Keya Chilka. A lovely woman adoring this Earth.

Trans people are quietly ostracized from friend groups and made as social pariahs in society. We are demonized, told we are disgusting, and found repulsive. Many people silently avoid us, scared of our bodies, our minds, and our ideology. Life is inherently unfair for us, Mom. It's unfair in every aspect of the word: unfair because we couldn't serve in the military under Trump, unfair because our teenagers can't get good healthcare, unfair because we are taunted and teased in school, and want to take our lives as a result. Unfair because we were born into the wrong body at birth, and suffer as a result–emotionally, mentally, physically, psychologically, even spiritually. It's unfair that we have worse dating lives–but people are slowly catching up to us. It's unfair that we have a harder time getting jobs if we don't pass well–and when we do pass well, we still encounter transphobia in the workplace.

Society is more fucked up than it is okay. I am sick of the injustices of the world, so much so that I want to take a hammer, bulldoze the neighborhood, and yell at the top of my lungs, while stringing a big, brown bottle of liquor and downing that past midnight. I want to rage against the man–against bigotry.

I GOT ANTHONY BOURDAIN'S initials tattooed on my back, Mom. *A.B.* Anthony fucking Bourdain.

He is a chef, a mastermind, a hero of unknown proportions. He describes his travels in boarding a three seater jet in the Congo in a thunderstorm, in a jet that will creak and make all sorts of haphazard noises. He was barely bombed in Lebanon on work travel there. He travels beyond borders–in fact, he made borders enmeshed into one, not caring what cultures exchanged hello's to reach other. He made culture a thing to love and not fear. And he made food a conduit for that to happen.

Mom, these words are all I have to offer you. You birthed me, fed me, watered me, read to me. Yet I am nothing but mutiny: misery on a winter day, dysfunction at all times. The literature I spoon through troves of words is my only valuable gift to God and God's Earth. Take words away from me, and there is no more life in my body. In my bones. I am a wretched creature. A monster. A narcissist and nihilist. A cynic, a skeptic at every turn. But I am also a writer, and I find beauty in the cacophony of verbs that will grace these pages. My words will lift people up, and not down. They will help and heal. So take them as you will. It is the only thing I can give to you, Mama. I have sabotaged everything else.

26

ISAAC. THE NAME means laughter in Hebrew, and everyone thinks I'm a Jew. We're not Jews, Mom. Dad is Lutheran, and you come from a family of Texas evangelicals. *Isaac.* The best name ever. A name suited for an intellectual–a high powered intellectual–kind of like Isaac Newton, Mama.

Isaac. The best part of my day–adopting a term that has the first three letters of *Isabel* but is a man's name at heart, one suited for a philosopher pondering Kant and a scientist about to discover the Periodic Table.

Isaac. Vagabond, renegade, rogue man of international mystery. These are the terms that define my new manhood. My passport sits in a cigar box full of Cubans and old ID cards. Someday I will join the Order of Malta and puff on Romeo and Juliets in a seaside town next to a gone mafia boss. But those are just wishes for now. Until then, I remain the most untacky human on the planet–the most sought after fetish one can hope for, except rarely anyone seeks after me. People crave comfort, they crave stereotypes, they crave other tacky people like them. People who listen to Taylor Swift and go to NFL games (*the pills in my bathroom cabinet are linebackers*). People who work in marketing and have two kids. Women who shop for purses on Etsy. Men who play fantasy basketball.

I am sick of tacky people. The world needs more folk like me, Mom. Folk who bend gender rules and play by our own guidelines. The world is full of walking prototypes–sorority girls popping a squat and frat kings making fun of others. Stop it with this nonsense. It's time to write literary critiques of Toni Morrison and push out poetry. It's time to fly to Moscow and buy a Putin propaganda shirt ironically.

I DON'T KNOW ANYTHING besides writing. The Earth is a wasteland where I get drunk through rum, vodka, IPAs. I get boozed up and ready to fight. If I'm not boozed up then I'm busy wrecking some relationship. When I'm not wrecking a relationship I'm at the strip club trying to find another one. I told you about the strip club. It does nothing good for me in the long run. I go there most nights, two, three times a week, and use my paychecks on Stellas and one dollar tips. The club gives me life, just for an hour or two, but sometimes I sit in that chair for three or four. The women have come to like me: I'm not threatening, I'm not sleazy, and I'm not an old creep.

I am sick of this disease eating my mind. I'm sick of the chance of being full blown manic for another year. I'm sick of the threat of psychosis looming on a nearby horizon–just waiting there, waiting to taunt and tease, pull and push, hit me with a fist to infinity. But most of all, I'm sick at the idea that I could lose it all one day, Mom–lose all of my marbles and be confined to a ward for the rest of my life, never able to talk to Helen, or Phoebe, or Dad again, or just seeing them in occasional visits, when I'm yelling at the walls and haphazardly pounding at the bed. I wouldn't know what was going on in Phoebe and Helen's lives–I wouldn't know which continents they were traveling to, which partners they were ensconced with, which new pets they owned, what their dreams and aspirations would be ten years from then. I wouldn't know which color nail polish they would be putting on. I wouldn't know what their hair would look like. I wouldn't know how they were feeling. I wouldn't know what kind of meals they were cooking at home. And I would survive on hospital food and a legacy of your wealth and a crazed brain.

So here, indeed, is where it comes to an end. This is the finish line, this is the part where drums beat and goodbyes are mouthed under a cascade of tears. This is the part when birds cry, when angels sing their last anthem, when God either takes us to heaven or to hell.

You have taken me to the world–to states, to regions, to countries. You have shown me politicians and vagabonds and broken souls. You have mouthed *I love you* two thousand and six times. You have given us brie, books, Harry Potter, film, Italy, Hillary Clinton, and a family.

But despite all of this–despite the humdrum of riches, the success on plaques, the awards strewn on the table, I have one thing left to say and one thing only, Mom:

I live in Hurt Capital.

ACKNOWLEDGMENTS

FIRST AND FOREMOST, I'd like to thank my family for this book, even though some members of it will not be happy that it is published, I will mention them nonetheless: Helen, Phoebe, Mom, Dad. Helen is my bedrock of support and has convinced me, over the years, that twin telepathy exists, whether she knows it or not. She helps me through crises even when I am hostile to her help, which is a mistake I never want to make again. I am proud of Phoebe for becoming the woman she is today: she is already succeeding professionally and is personally successful as well. To me, Phoebe is a role model of confidence, and I think of her whenever I need to be more composed. I'd like to thank Mom for many things: first, for being the recipient of this letter-turned book, and second for showing me strength during weak times. Lastly, I'd like to thank Dad for treating me like a son, which means, at times, being more hard on me, in hopes of molding me into a more responsible man. Dad: I will never be like you—I will never be a CEO—but I do try.

I'd like to thank an old Yale friend, India June, for dozens, if not hundreds, of phone calls over the last few years. India has supported me through bipolar and even offers fairly accurate suggestions on ways to medically treat, or at least perceive, the disease. She is the person who was on the phone with me when I sought out inpatient treatment, and encouraged me to seek hospitalization.

India is open and celebratory of neurodivergence, and is training to be a doctor one day. She will make an exemplary one, and she has already done an exemplary job of serving in the US Navy.

I'd like to thank Sonali Shukla for being a good friend as well. Phone conversations with you, in spite of the difference between DC and Seattle, are enlightening and make my day.

I'd like to acknowledge Joshua Davis, who I enlisted to help me arrange a finished draft manuscript into cogent chapters (or rather uncogent chapters, since the prose is beautifully chaotic). Our motto between each other was, aptly, "chaos preferred". He jokingly mentioned that our little slogan would be received well on t-shirts, and I agree. Josh has edited my poetry in the past, and is a beautiful poet himself. I trust him, more than anyone else, with tweaking and reflecting on prose. His knack for eliminating redundancy is in high demand. I envy his eloquent style, and he carries a gift on his shoulders that most others don't have. I would love to refer him as an editor to anyone in need.

I'd like to thank three more family members: my Abuelita, who is 96, and still texts us grandchildren in sophisticated paragraphs and sees us through FaceTime calls. Abuelita is our matriarch and queen. Uncle Eric, my father's brother, has taken me on great text conversations, where we talk about anything ranging from the power of AI to the brown bears that materialize in his Los Angeles backyard. Aunt Laura, my father's sister, offers the family dozens of bouts of comedic relief, through great jokes, and more stress relieving stories about her life in Chicago.

I'd like to thank a few professors who taught me at Yale: Cynthia Zarin, Anne Fadiman, Michael Cunningham, and Charles HIll. Professor Hill has since passed, but he was one of the gentlest, most compassionate older men I met at Yale. He let me amend my senior thesis too many times, starting off with Obama's failure of a red line policy on Syria, to other myriad things. Professor Zarin and I had a love-hate relationship. I vividly remember engaging in a shouting match with her in a Jonathan Edwarfs stairwell, over my lack of attendance to her essays class, and that somehow was one of my favorite memories at Yale. Professor Cunningham won a Pulitzer for "The Hours" and has probably forgotten who I am. But he made his creative writing seminar feel like a hobby–and not a graded, stressful class–and that was a present I didn't expect from such a high caliber professional. Meanwhile, professor Fadiman and I have kept in brief contact over the years, and if it weren't for her and her personal memoir class, I probably wouldn't be writing this today.

There is one doctor in DC who has been treating me since 2017 and, in my recovery from a year of mania, proved to be exceptionally brilliant and helpful in a way that I wouldn't have foreseen. I will not name him here, but we share one similar accolade in life.

I'd like to thank the staff of the Yale Daily News, both then and now, for publishing my pieces and letting me write in a way where I don't have to dumb down my prose for other mainstream outlets. The YDN allows one to tinker with brilliance, to the heart's content. Other publications don't allow that.

Lastly–but certainly not least–I'd like to thank my ex-wife, Keya Chilka, for the endless love and support she showed me for five years (and many more, to this day). Keya's love helped me in becoming a better and more morally conscientious person–she made me part of a community, and helped self regulate the roller-coaster of wild emotions that bipolar entails. It is unconventional to mention ex-spouses in these sections, but I feel compelled to, and I am endlessly thankful for her warmth and guidance. Our marriage didn't work out, but our appreciation and love for each other continues to this day. I'm glad we can have open conversations about the pain we were both feeling in recent years. We certainly felt a lot of it—almost too much. Her review of this manuscript is what spurred me to finally send it to an agent.

www.ingramcontent.com/pod-product-compliance
Ingram Content Group UK Ltd.
Pitfield, Milton Keynes, MK11 3LW, UK
UKHW021123170325
456354UK00009B/725

9 798822 979277